R. RUSSELL BIXLER

UNBREAKABLE PROMISES

HOW TO KNOW—AND RECEIVE— ALL THAT GOD HAS GIVEN YOU

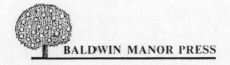

BALDWIN MANOR PRESS

UNBREAKABLE PROMISES:
How to Know—and Receive—*All* that God Has Given You

Copyright © 1987 by R. Russell Bixler
Published by Baldwin Manor Press
4722 Baptist Road
Pittsburgh, Pennsylvania 15227
All rights reserved
Unless otherwise identified, scripture quotations in this book
are from the *Revised Standard Version*.
Manuscript typed by Ruth Coles
Artwork by Waltraud Hendel

ISBN 0-9617094-1-3

DEDICATION

To David Noel Freedman, one of the world's leading Old Testament scholars, who 24 years ago lighted a fire within my heart in his graduate class entitled, "The Covenant."

And to my sweet Norma, who patiently wonders if it may really be true that "of making many books there is no end."

CONTENTS

FOREWORD

Who knows what Christ's Church could have accomplished had the Church held to its convenantal roots and relationships, rather than compromising with Greek philosophies?

Having taught a college-level course in Bible Covenants for several years, I am convinced that improper understanding of the covenants has resulted in weakness and confusion in the Church. Dispensationalism claims to be "rightly dividing" the word, but dispenses with the covenants as being "Jewish." Covenant theologians find an "old" covenant and a "new" covenant, with its blessings exclusively Christian. Catholicism proclaims the Roman Church to be the Kingdom and the Israel of God. The answer to the confusion is found in a scriptural approach to the covenants.

Russ Bixler brings fresh insight to the scriptures; he digs countless promises out of the Word. His provocative book could spark a repentant return to our biblical, covenantal relationship with Almighty God. His writing is complete, but not complicated. It is readable and quite inspiring.

My prayer is that *Unbreakable Promises* will have a wide readership.

Charles Trombley
Broken Arrow, Oklahoma
Evangelist, missionary, teacher,
popular television personality.
Author of eight books.

PREFACE

God speaks to us in language we understand. I have never heard the Lord speak in my spirit in Spanish, or Latin, or even in King James English. When He speaks to me, the Lord may even use a very personal expression that I use in my everyday speech.

God also speaks to us in *forms* we understand. He has never talked to me about a Shinto temple: that is not a part of my experience. He has never spoken to me about obedience to the British colonial law: that has not been a part of my family's experience since Britain granted independence to Pennsylvania and the other twelve colonies in 1783.

Rather, the Lord talks to us in today's English language about today's relationships in today's world. So has He always done. The Bible records just such a pattern in God's dealing with his People through the ages—whether in Adam's day, or Abraham's day, or King David's, or the Apostle Paul's. He speaks to every generation differently— according to their language, their customs, their needs, and their hopes.

Yet, there is one quality common to every age of human existence, whether in 4000 B.C. or A.D. 2000. We humans must have covenants. People's behavior must be agreed upon among ourselves, in covenants, or we suffocate in chaos. We agree in mutual covenants that murder is crimi- nal, that traffic lights are to be obeyed, and that a business- man's covenant to deliver a certain product for a certain price is to be honored. Such covenants have been understood from the very beginning of human history. And God is quite aware of this fact.

God also believes in covenants. Thus He, too, consistently deals with us in such relationships—and in varying forms that always seem to fit succeeding generations and new cultures. *The covenants unify the Bible*! Covenants between God and man are the intertwining strands that hold the Bible together from Genesis through Revelation.

We will follow these cords of divine-human covenants where they lead us, revealing a great deal about God, as well as some surprising blessings in our relationship with Him. The biblical covenants are quite spectacular when seen together, in proper order. This book will provide a breathtaking picture of Almighty God's agreements with man—in a sense, perhaps, a God's-eye view of the whole story of the dealings between Creator and creature. First-hand knowledge of the biblical covenants, then, will enable the reader to claim all the gifts God has given to his children. The blood of Jesus Christ provides us with far more than we realize.

The narrative builds gradually toward a cataclysmic confrontation between the two conflicting covenant traditions of the Old Testament. Suddenly, a destructive explosion-and-failure threatens the very purposes of God. Then begins God's dramatic unraveling of these tangled strands of covenant, followed by his creative re-weaving into precious cords of unending blessing. Even today, the ever-alive biblical covenants point to some fascinating prophetic occurrences scheduled by God for the exciting times just ahead of us.

Scripture quotations are, unless otherwise noted, taken from the *Revised Standard Version*. Old Testament dating is based upon the traditional (biblical) chronology; modern revised dating of the Exodus hinges upon a faulty Egyptian chronology that has no firm anchor in history.

The Ancient Jews Object to Christianity

The ancient (A.D. 170) Greek philosopher Celsus wrote a book entitled *True Doctrine*. Celsus devoted all his efforts toward ridiculing the foolishness of Christianity. "These Christians," he scoffed, "love each other even before they are acquainted!" And thereby Celsus pinned an unintended badge of merit upon every Christian he knew.

Celsus also quoted a Jew who was complaining about Christians:

> "Why do you Christians take your origin from our Jewish religion, and then, as if you are progressing in knowledge, despise our things, although you have no other origin for your doctrine than our Law? . . . What is wrong with you Christians that you left the Law of our fathers, and being deluded by this Jesus, you were quite ludicrously deceived and have deserted us for another name and the practices of another life?"
>
> (Origen, *Against Celsus*, II,1)

In a fierce debate a generation earlier, Trypho the Jew had also complained bitterly to Justin, one of the early Church fathers:

> "You Christians openly despise the Covenant, neglect the laws which follow from it, and you attempt to persuade yourselves that you know God, even though you perform none of those things that God-fearing Jews do!"
>
> (Justin, *Dialogue with Trypho*, 10)

Christians of Gentile (non-Jewish) heritage, making up per-haps 95% of the second-century Church, could seldom answer these objections effectively. Most Gentile Christians of this period (and ever since) did not understand the ques-tions those Jews were asking, and our responses through the centuries have usually missed the mark.

First, the opposition and persecution from Jewish leaders in the early centuries was often violent, even irrational, lead-ing to much suffering and death for Christians. Trypho the Jew, Justin's debating opponent quoted above, finally in anger accused his enemy to the Roman authorities, leading to Justin's death and subsequent title, Justin Martyr. Jewish families were often shattered as some members realized that Jesus of Nazareth was indeed the Messiah, while others were dissuaded by their rabbis, who usually rejected Jesus with-out investigation. But further, and perhaps more important, Gentile Christians approached the Jewish God boldly through Jesus Christ, bypassing totally the Old Testament, the covenants, the Law, the synagogue and the practices of Judaism. Christians of A.D. 170, except for those with a background in Judaism, did not understand how the Jews perceived their God.

To this day we still must approach God through his Son, the Lord Jesus Christ. But nearly all of us have come to know Jesus personally simply by accepting Him as Lord, in faith, seldom seeing Him through the Old Testament. The Gen-tile Christian has rarely concerned himself with the Old Testament covenants. The ancient Jew, however, was accustomed to a living God who made *covenants! laws! agreements! promises!* Christians today know they have been saved, but they rarely understand their salvation in terms of "covenant," as the Bible describes. As a further result, *Christians seldom realize their privileges in the Kingdom of God.* This book answers that need.

So the Christian Church of the second century could hardly respond properly to Celsus' Jew, or Trypho the Jew, when they asked their challenging questions. This book also seeks out the biblical responses to these honest Jewish objections, presenting the beliefs held by a first or second century Jew who had experienced salvation through Jesus Christ. Our study will help us to understand the message of Paul and the other Jewish Christians when they witnessed of Jesus in the various synagogues and, further, why the response by the Jews was so often violent. And finally, we will learn a lot more about who we are in Jesus Christ, and all our glorious privileges through his precious blood.

Our modern lack of understanding of the biblical covenants is further complicated by what is termed "covenant theology" in Protestant Christendom. In sixteenth century Geneva, Switzerland, the Reformer, John Calvin, sharply distinguished between the 39 books he called the "Old Covenant," or "Old Testament," and the 27 books which he termed the "New Covenant," or "New Testament." Calvinist teachings said that God made a covenant with Adam in the Garden of Eden; Adam broke that "old" covenant, and he and his descendants suffered the consequences of God's wrath. Jesus Christ, the second Adam, atoned for man's sin; God then established another covenant, known as the New Covenant. Thus the two "covenants" of covenant theology.

Such a teaching is not quite correct. The word "covenant" does not appear in God's recorded dealings with Adam. There is no "agreement" between the parties of Genesis 2; no one—neither God nor man—is described as having bound himself by a covenant promise. Nor may we legitimately claim even an "implicit" covenant in the Garden of Eden. Therefore, the exaggerated division between Old and New Testaments created by Calvinistic (Reformed) "covenant theology" is somewhat misleading.

Nor is the Bible limited to just two covenants, as pictured by the Calvinists. There are actually six biblical covenants between God and man. These six covenants are much richer and more fascinating than the Reformed theologians thought, and God's plan and pattern are wonderfully revealed by a more careful study of the Bible. We must let the Bible speak for itself.

The Covenant Society

All of human society operates on the basis of covenants. "Covenant" is roughly synonymous with words such as agreement, treaty, contract, deed, testament, will, commitment, bargain. A covenant occurs between two parties or groups of parties who agree to perform in certain ways. A dentist agrees to fill his patient's tooth, for which the patient agrees to pay the dentist a certain amount of money. A political candidate covenants to do certain things if the voters place him in office. Severe difficulties in the community or nation begin whenever the officeholder treats that covenant with contempt. The traffic light represents a stipulation derived from a larger covenant, and terrible consequences occur when numbers of citizens (parties to that covenant) begin disobeying traffic signals. Human civilization is impossible without covenants that are respected.

Further, human covenants are always *bilateral*. That is, two or more people agree among themselves on certain actions as, for example, If you do so-and-so, then I (or, we) will do thus-and-so. All human covenants are thus bilateral, or multilateral—conditional upon all parties performing as agreed.

All except one. There is one form of *unilateral* covenant in human behavior, with no conditions required, no responses demanded. That one unilateral covenant is the relationship established the moment a mother sees her newborn baby. The mother (with the father) makes a unilateral, unconditional promise to that baby to love, feed, house and care for him or her. No questions asked; no conditions demanded.

But this covenant love of a parent is the exception. All other covenants between humans are conditional upon the behavior of both parties.

Biblical history describes various bilateral covenants between people. Jacob and his father-in-law, Laban, agreed upon a covenant in Gen. 31:44-54. David and Jonathan covenanted with each other in brotherly love (1 Samuel 18:3). The kings of Israel and Syria entered into an ill-fated covenant of mutual defense against Assyria (Isaiah 7:1,2). Covenants are found throughout biblical history. The Hebrew word *berith* ("covenant") appears 290 times in the Old Testament.

God honors that absolute need for covenants in human relationships. Since He deals with us in terms we can understand, He too establishes covenants with his People. God alone has the prerogative of initiating or accepting an agreement between Himself and a man, a nation, or the human race. Man cannot guarantee that God will agree to a particular covenant proposed by any human. Thus, the true biblical covenants are the six that *God* has ordained between man and Himself. These six biblical covenants have profoundly affected all of human history, the children of Israel primarily, but also the rest of mankind.

I

The Bilateral Covenant

Our study of the biblical covenants begins in ancient Egypt. There God found his People Israel in bondage about 3,500 years ago. As recorded in Exodus, He brought the Hebrews out of Egypt with a mighty display of power. Gathering them together at the foot of a mountain in the Sinai wilderness, the LORD there established a Covenant with Israel.

How does God establish a covenant with men?

First, the LORD proclaims his covenant to (and perhaps through) a particular man, one chosen person, such as Moses, or David. Second, He frames his covenant in terms that men can understand, in language and stipulations taken from their own human experience.

There were actual earthly models for such a human-divine covenant in 1500 B.C., models which apparently were well-known throughout the Near East. So God patterned his covenant at Sinai after the widely used "suzerainty" treaty of the Hittites, although this type of treaty-covenant was common in the Near East long before the Hittite Empire became an international force. We use the Hittites as an example because the best archaeological remains are from their culture; they left us a big royal library which includes some of these detailed treaties.

The Hittite Empire of 1500 B.C. was centered in an area we call today eastern Turkey. The Hittites had conquered some adjacent smaller nations, placing puppet rulers over these subject peoples. Often the vassal (puppet) ruler was a member of the royal household of the conquered nation. The victorious king (suzerain) of the Hittite Empire would establish a *personal* covenant between himself and the puppet ruler. Archaeology has shown us that the Hittite suzerainty covenant normally followed this outline.*

(1) PREAMBLE, such as, "These are the words of . . . ";

(2) PROLOGUE, the reciting of past relationships and favors by the suzerain to the vassal ruler;

(3) STIPULATIONS, the conditions accepted by the vassal ruler;

(4) RULES FOR DEPOSIT AND PUBLIC READING;

(5) LIST OF WITNESSES, including all the gods of the suzerain and the gods of the vassal ruler;

(6) BLESSINGS AND CURSES, all of which were normally only *religious*; no human sanctions were mentioned, only the blessing or punishment of the gods for obedience or disobedience.

There is an excellent biblical example of a suzerainty covenant described in Ezekiel 17:11-21. King Nebuchadnezzar of Babylon had captured Jerusalem the first time in 598 B.C. He took the king of Judah, 18-year-old Jehoiachin, to Babylonian exile along with a sizable number of artisans and other skilled workers. Nebuchadnezzar placed Jehoiachin's uncle, Mattaniah (whom he renamed Zedekiah), on the throne as his puppet ruler of Judah. Nebuchadnezzar (the suzerain) then required the new King Zedekiah to submit to a personal covenant, insisting that his oath be taken in the name of the God of Judah.

---

* Adapted from G. E. Mendenhall, *Law and Covenant in Israel and the Ancient Near East,* Pittsburgh: The Biblical Colloquium, 1955, pp. 32-34.

Several years later the puppet King Zedekiah, excited by a short-lived revolution in Babylon and unrest in theconquered nations, and relying upon the empty promises of the Egyptian pharaoh, led Judah in rebellion against the Babylonian king.

Through the prophet Ezekiel, God spoke harshly to Judah's king about his impending punishment, because Zedekiah had profaned the name of the LORD when he broke his oath to Nebuchadnezzar. The Babylonian king had been careful to require Zedekiah to take the oath of the suzerainty covenant in the name of Judah's God, the God Zedekiah feared. The reader may wish to examine the full story in Ezekiel 17:11-21; this narrative helps us to understand the structure of God's Covenant established with Israel at Sinai.

The Mosaic Covenant

The establishment of the Sinai Covenant is depicted in Exodus 19 and 20 (partially repeated in Deut. 5). Since Moses was God's human intermediary, it is normally called the Mosaic Covenant. The basic provisions of this Covenant we have entitled the "Ten Commandments," or, the "Decalogue." The resemblance of the Mosaic Covenant to the Hittite suzerainty covenants is striking; all of the essential qualities of this ancient secular covenant are found in the Mosaic Covenant and some of its derivative ordinances. Thus we see God speaking to the Israelites in language they understood and dealing with them through a style of covenant with which they were familiar.

A notable difference between the Hittite suzerainty covenants and the Mosaic Covenant is that the Hittite covenants were established between human rulers (to be enforced by the gods), while the Covenant at Sinai was established between God and a nation (to be enforced by that nation).

Not everyone agrees upon the correct numbering of the basic stipulations of the Mosaic Covenant, the Ten Commandments. Today we have three different numberings for the Decalogue—the traditional Jewish, the Protestant, and the Roman Catholic (with some Lutherans). The three possible numberings of the Ten Commandments are as follows, from Exodus 20, verses 2 through 17.

The Ten Commandments listed by verses			
	Jewish	*Protestant*	*Catholic*
(1)	2	3	3-6
(2)	3-6	4-6	7
(3)	7	7	8-11
(4)	8-11	8-11	12
(5)	12	12	13
(6)	13	13	14
(7)	14	14	15
(8)	15	15	16
(9)	16	16	17a
(10)	17	17	17b

The Protestant numbering divides Commandments One and Two at what may be the middle of a sentence, as the Catholic numbering also divides its last two at the middle of verse 17. The traditional Jewish numbering considers verse two, God's self-identification, as Commandment One. The Jewish scheme appears to be correct, and, in addition, it best conforms to the Hittite suzerainty covenant. Let's examine the ancient suzerainty formula as it appears in Exodus 20.

(1) PREAMBLE:

"And God spoke all these words . . . "
(Exodus 20:1)

(2) PROLOGUE:

"I am the LORD your God, who brought you out of the land of Egypt, out of the house of bondage."
(Exodus 20:2)

(3) STIPULATIONS:

"You shall have no other gods before me. You shall not make for yourself a graven image, or any likeness of anything that is in heaven above, or that is in the earth beneath, or that is in the water under the earth; you shall not bow down to them or serve them, for I the LORD your God am a jealous God, visiting the iniquity of the fathers upon the children to the third and the fourth generation of those who hate me, but showing steadfast love to thousands of those who love me and keep my commandments.

"You shall not take the name of the LORD your God in vain; for the LORD will not hold him guiltless who takes his name in vain.

"Remember the sabbath day, to keep it holy. Six days you shall labor, and do all your work; but the seventh day is a sabbath to the LORD your God; in it you shall not do any work, you, or your son, or your daughter, your manservant, or your maidservant, or your cattle, or the sojourner who is within your gates; for in six days the LORD made heaven and earth, the sea, and all that is in them, and rested the seventh day; therefore the LORD blessed the sabbath day and hallowed it.

"Honor your father and your mother, that your days may be long in the land which the LORD your God gives you.

"You shall not kill.

"You shall not commit adultery.

"You shall not steal.

"You shall not bear false witness against your neighbor.

"You shall not covet your neighbor's house; you shall not covet your neighbor's wife, or his man-servant, or his maidservant, or his ox, or his ass, or anything that is your neighbor's."

(Exodus 20:3-17)

The remaining parts of the suzerainty covenant formula are found elsewhere in the Pentateuch.

(4) DEPOSIT AND PUBLIC READING:

Then he took the book of the covenant, and read it in the hearing of the people; and they said, "All that the LORD has spoken we will do, and we will be obedient."

(Exodus 24:7)

"Three times in the year you shall keep a feast to me. You shall keep the feast of unleavened bread . . . You shall keep the feast of harvest . . . You shall keep the feast of ingathering at the end of the year . . . Three times in the year shall all your males appear before the Lord God."
(Exodus 23:14-17)

And Moses commanded them, "At the end of every seven years, at the set time of the year of release, at the feast of booths, when all Israel comes to appear before the Lord your God at the place which he will choose, you shall read this law before all Israel in their hearing. Assemble the people, men, women, and little ones, and the sojourner within your towns, that they may hear and learn to fear the Lord your God, and be careful to do all the words of this law, and that their children, who have not known it, may hear and learn to fear the Lord your God, as long as you live in the land which you are going over the Jordan to possess."
(Deut. 31:10-13)

(5) LIST OF WITNESSES:

"I call heaven and earth to witness against you this day, that I have set before you life and death, blessing and curse; therefore choose life, that you and your descendants may live, loving the Lord your God, obeying his voice, and cleaving to him; for that means life to you and length of days, that you may dwell in the land which the Lord swore to your fathers, to Abraham, to Isaac, and to Jacob, to give them."
(Deut. 30:19,20)

(6) BLESSINGS AND CURSES:

"And if you obey the voice of the LORD your God, being careful to do all his commandments which I command you this day, the LORD your God will set you high above all the nations of the earth. And all these blessings shall come upon you and overtake you, if you obey the voice of the LORD your God."   (Deut. 28:1,2)

The promised blessings for obedience continue in detail through Deut. 28:14. The curses for disobedience begin at verse 15 and continue until the end of this very long chapter. They are frightening, and one of the curses for disobedience is especially noteworthy and quite prophetic.

"And the LORD will scatter you among all peoples, from one end of the earth to the other; and there you shall serve other gods, of wood and stone, which neither you nor your fathers have known. And among these nations you shall find no ease, and there shall be no rest for the sole of your foot; but the LORD will give you there a trembling heart, and failing eyes, and a languishing soul."   (Deut. 28:64,65)

And the Jews have indeed been scattered "from one end of the earth to the other" because of their persistent violation of the bilateral, conditional, Mosaic Covenant.

The Inauguration of the Mosaic Covenant

The LORD first asked the Israelites, through Moses, if they wished to participate in the Covenant.

"You have seen what I did to the Egyptians, and how I bore you on eagles' wings and brought you to myself. Now therefore, if you will obey my voice and keep my covenant, you shall be my own possession among all peoples; for all the earth is mine, and you shall be to me a kingdom of priests and a holy nation . . ."

So Moses came and called the elders of the people, and set before them all these words which the LORD had commanded him. And all the people answered together and said, "All that the LORD has spoken we will do." And Moses reported the words of the people to the LORD.

(Exodus 19:4-8)

More than mere agreement was required to seal a biblical covenant. The shedding of sacrificial blood was also necessary: "Hence even the first [Mosaic] covenant was not ratified without blood" (Hebrews 9:18). So Moses

. . . rose early in the morning, and built an altar at the foot of the mountain, and twelve pillars, according to the twelve tribes of Israel. And he sent young men of the people of Israel, who offered burnt offerings and sacrificed peace offerings of oxen to the LORD. And Moses took half of the blood and put it in basins, and half of the blood he threw against the altar. Then he took the book

> of the covenant, and read it in the hearing of the
> people; and they said, "All that the LORD has
> spoken we will do, and we will be obedient." And
> Moses took the blood and threw it upon the
> people, and said, "Behold the blood of the cove-
> nant which the LORD has made with you in accor-
> dance with all these words."   (Exodus 24:4-8)

This picture demonstrates how blood was normally shed
to ratify a biblical covenant between God and man. An oath
was also taken, and customarily the parties ate the sacrificial meal together as a further sealing of the covenant.

> Then Moses and Aaron, Nadab, and Abihu, and
> seventy of the elders of Israel went up, and they
> saw the God of Israel; and there was under his feet
> as it were a pavement of sapphire stone, like the
> very heaven for clearness. And he did not lay his
> hand on the chief men of the people of Israel; they
> beheld God, and ate and drank.
>   (Exodus 24:9-11)

Ordinarily the 70 elders would have died from beholding
God, but the LORD was endorsing their eating in his presence; after all, He was the One who had invited them to
dinner. God Himself had initiated the establishment of the
Mosaic Covenant.

This is one of those uncommon occurrences when
Almighty God, the Creator of the universe, humbled Himself before men. In fact, we will find that those momentous
occasions when the LORD was ratifying most of the six
biblical covenants were the moments He was condescend-
ing to meet man at the human level. They are truly among
the great occasions in all of divine-human history.

After Israel accepted the Mosaic Covenant, God restated and enlarged upon his commitment to them.

> And he said, "Behold, I make a covenant. Before all your people I will do marvels, such as have not been wrought in all the earth or in any nation; and all the people among whom you are shall see the work of the LORD; for it is a terrible thing that I will do with you." . . . And the LORD said to Moses, "Write these words; in accordance with these words I have made a covenant with you and with Israel." (Exodus 34:10,27)

When God asserted that He would do a "terrible thing," He meant a terrible thing to his enemies. He was "the living God," powerful and avenging. The LORD was understood in the Old Testament as a militant God, the LORD God of hosts. The "hosts" are the warring angels of heaven. He was a mighty God who fights victoriously against his enemies.

He was truly a God to be feared—in a very real sense, God the Enemy.

God had cursed the earth because of Adam and Eve's sin. He had cursed the human race. He had cursed the earth. He was an angry God. He was so angry that He destroyed all of mankind except for Noah and his family, and, in addition, severely degraded the earth's climate following the Flood. When the Tower of Babel was built, God came down and scattered the people and confused their speech. The Sodom and Gomorrah destruction was clearly the work of an angry God. Men lived in terror of spiritual powers. Thus He was perceived in Moses' day.

We barely see the first glimmers of the love of God being manifested when He moved in the life of Abraham.

Somewhat more of his love appears in God's relationship with Israel in the wilderness. But not until the prophet Hosea (750 B.C.) is the word "love" used extensively about the LORD. And finally, the full revelation of the loving God came in Jesus Christ.

This angry God was to be feared and to be appeased. *All* the peoples of 1500 B.C. were terrified of their pagan gods—gods who were depicted as planetary deities—Mercury, Venus, Mars, Jupiter, Saturn, the sun and the moon, and, in addition, the earthly demonic spirits. After all, this battered earth had already suffered a terrible series of catastrophic events from the heavens, such as Noah's Flood and the Sodom-Gomorrah destruction, and other devastations that the Old Testament records. So pagan man's religious duties consisted primarily of appeasing these hostile and dangerous gods and spirits of the world of nature.

But in the Mosaic Covenant with Israel, the one true God who had created the heavens and the earth, indeed, had created all of nature, was setting his people free from that prison of polytheism, although He was still to be feared and placated with sacrifices. The LORD God was allowing his Chosen People to worship Him in ways they could understand.

The Israelites were accustomed to pagan neighbors who, in their worship, honored gods and goddesses who were capricious and vindictive. These pagan deities supposedly demanded extensive sacrifice and service. Polytheistic nations established elaborate sacrificial covenants with their gods, requiring a great deal of time, effort, expense, wasted food, even human life. Modern archaeological digs in ancient pagan communities regularly uncover vast amounts of evidence of the all-consuming job of placating the heathen gods and spirits. But the true Creator-God of Israel didn't require such extravagance for Himself.

> "If I were hungry, I would not tell you; for the
> world and all that is in it is mine."
>
> (Psalms 50:12)

And, as the Apostle Paul described Him,

> "Nor is he served by human hands, as though he
> needed anything, since he himself gives to all men
> life and breath and everything."   (Acts 17:25)

The food from the sacrifices to the LORD was largely to be
consumed by the priests, the Levites and the worshipers
together.

We observe that the Mosaic Covenant, with its Ten Commandments, was a strong reaction against paganism. As has
been noted, pagan religion is the struggle of man to deal
with hostile and demonic spiritual forces. Humans always
feel uncomfortable whenever they are not in control of their
own destiny. So all of pagan religion must consist of
continuing attempts to appease, manipulate and control the
unseen spiritual powers in charge of this earth, forces that
ever seem to threaten mankind's welfare. Since we are told
authoritatively that "the whole world is in the power of the
evil one" (1 John 5:19), and, as Satan told Jesus on the Mount
of Temptation, the whole earth "has been delivered to me,
and I give it to whom I will" (Luke 4:6), we Christians are
aware that these gods, goddesses, spirits, principalities and
powers are indeed evil, standing in opposition to the Creator, the real God and Father of our Lord Jesus Christ. But
one who is not a believing Christian can hardly know this
truth.

Sacrifices are considered by pagan man to be effective
means of appeasement. He thinks, Now my god owes me
some favors! In addition, the making of images or pictures,

or some sort of representation of deity, gives the pagan worshiper a sense of power over his god: He has made or purchased the image himself, he can watch it, feel it, move it, care for it, control it; he *owns* the idol. Although he knows very well that the image is not really the god (who is spirit), the pagan feels less vulnerable and more in control of his own life and the world immediately about him. Read about Rachel's stealing her father Laban's household gods, and this will become clearer (Gen. 31:17-35).

The Ten Commandments

1. *I am the* LORD*, your God.*

"I am the LORD your God, who brought you out of the land of Egypt, out of the house of bondage."
(Exodus 20:2)

The First Commandment the LORD gave to Israel set them free from this ages-long bondage. He was saying something like this: "I am Yahweh, your God! You need not appease the gods of this world, so worship Me alone! You will worship me, the Creator, rather than the creation! I will not be manipulated or coerced! I am the living God!"

The LORD had already condescended to reveal to Moses (and thus to all Israel) his very own personal Name, Yahweh. In fact, the *only* truths man can know about the real God are those truths that He has chosen to reveal to us.

"The secret things belong to the LORD our God; but the things that are revealed belong to us and to our children for ever."
(Deut. 29:29)

By worshiping the one true Creator-God who is Spirit, we are set free from being concerned about appeasing the elemental spirits of this world (see Col. 2:20). Thus, as we realize how meaningful and precious this truth is to us today, we can perceive how blessed were the ancient Israelites at the foot of Mt. Sinai.

Still, there is within all of us this deep urge to be in control of our own destinies. Adam and Eve succumbed to such a temptation, and ever since that fateful moment in the Garden of Eden, we their descendants have also been trying to make ourselves into little gods—in control of our own destinies. This urge often manifests itself in what the Bible calls "idolatry." During Moses' 40-day absence on Mt. Sinai, it was only a matter of days before Aaron, under pressure from the people, made a golden calf to represent the God who had brought Israel out of Egypt (Exodus 32; see also 1 Kings 12:28). The people really didn't see anything wrong with what they did. They were simply accustomed to portraying God with a physical image that described the LORD's attributes. The young bull that Aaron fashioned characterized (1) strength, (2) virility, (3) fierceness and (4) victory in warfare. The Israelites must have been quite bewildered at Moses' angry reaction when he came down from the mountain.

This deep-seated urge to practice false religion cursed God's Chosen People for the next thousand years, until finally the Babylonian Captivity broke that innate pagan spirit. At the heart of biblical theology, then, we see God's deep hostility to images. In fact, one of the two outstanding teachings of the Old Testament is that God is personal, and the personal God hates man-made images of Himself. (The other primary truth of the Old Testament is that man is sinful).

The Ten Commandments were both customary and revolutionary in the Near Eastern world of 1500 B.C. Some of the rules were similar to neighboring pagan law codes; others were quite new and startling.

As we have noted, the traditional Jewish numbering is probably correct, in which verse two, the LORD's self-identification, constitutes the opening statement, or, as the Bible itself says, the First of the "Ten Words" (Deut. 4:13).

> "I am the LORD your God, who brought you out of the land of Egypt, out of the house of bondage."
> (Exodus 20:2)

According to the Jewish counting, that initial statement is Commandment One, which means that there are really only nine "Commandments" as we today would consider them. We shall deal with them on that basis.

2. *You Shall Have No Other Gods Before Me.*

> "You shall have no other gods before me. You shall not make for yourself a graven image, or any likeness of anything that is in heaven above, or that is in the earth beneath, or that is in the water under the earth; you shall not bow down to them or serve them; for I the LORD your God am a jealous God, visiting the iniquity of the fathers upon the children to the third and the fourth generation of those who hate me, but showing steadfast love to thousands of those who love me and keep my commandments."
> (Exodus 20:3-6)

It has been suggested that the correct rendering of Exodus 20:3,4 is as follows.

"You shall have no other gods before me, not making for yourself a graven image, etc. . . . "

Thus, verse four would begin with a dependent clause, not a sentence complete in itself. If so, these two verses would properly be a single sentence, underscoring the Jewish (and Catholic) belief that it is all one Commandment, rather than the Protestant division into two.

This Commandment was the most radical of them all. Surely everybody knew that all worshipers must have physical representations of deity! In defense of idolaters, no one actually believes that the image is the god, but rather, the image *represents* the god, and, perhaps, houses the god, or provides a resting place upon which the god stands or sits. Even idolaters realize that all gods are spiritual. But the God of Abraham, Isaac and Jacob was trying to set Israel free from the terrible bondage of paganism, although the innate desire to possess religious images remained very strong in Israel. Not only were they not to make images of other gods, they were not to make images of the LORD either. This radical Commandment continued to be a source of bitter reaction and misunderstanding in Israel for a thousand years. Idolaters and prophets are natural enemies.

The writing prophets, from Amos (760 B.C.) to Jeremiah (587 B.C.), were in repeated trouble with their fellow countrymen over this issue. Let's learn from an imaginary dialogue between a prophet and a priest. The angry prophet is speaking out against an image used in worship, say, one of the two golden calves set up by the evil King Jeroboam I of Israel (1 Kings 12:28,29).

Prophet: "God is going to judge Israel for worshiping this golden calf!"

> *Priest:* "How can you make that terrible statement? We don't worship that calf! We worship the Lord, whom the calf represents!"
>
> *Prophet:* "But the Commandment says, 'You shall not make for yourself a graven image!' "
>
> *Priest:* "But that only refers to *other* gods, not to the Lord!"
>
> *Prophet:* "No! The Lord says you shall not make *any* graven images! He hates images of himself!"
>
> *Priest:* "Go prophesy somewhere else! You are desecrating this holy place with your blasphemous language against the Lord!"

By this time a number of pious worshipers have seized the prophet and are dragging him out of the sanctuary, deeply offended by the prophet's message. Soon he will be beaten severely, perhaps even killed. For one of the most dangerous acts a man can commit is to challenge another man's idols; the reaction can be violent.

This hypothetical story (see, however, Amos 7:10-17) indicates how strong is the "religious" spirit in man, and it demonstrates how revolutionary the First Commandment was—and still is! "Religious" people simply cannot perceive the idolatry in their hearts, even to this day. Several of the writing prophets predicted that just such idolatry was to be the major cause of God's judgment upon his People—first, the destruction and dispersal of the northern tribes in 721 B.C., and second, the destruction of Jerusalem and the Babylonian exile of Judah in 587 B.C.

But good came from that second tragedy; it was a humbled and chastened remnant that began straggling back to the Promised Land a generation later. Idolatry was never again as severe a problem as it had been for a thousand years.

Ironically, this Second Commandment describes a universal truth—that the idolater often goes unpunished (in this life), while his grandchildren and great grandchildren suffer the consequences.

> "I the LORD your God am a jealous God, visiting the iniquity of the fathers upon the children to the third and the fourth generation of those who hate me."   (Exodus 20:5)

Here is an inexorable law of our natural world, that later generations suffer for the sins of the fathers. A biblical example: Sixth century B.C. Judah was decimated and driven into Babylonian exile because of the sins of the seventh century King Manasseh. The evil, idolatrous Manasseh, according to 2 Kings 21:10-15, was the direct cause of the incredible suffering of his great grandchildren. Lamentations underscores the tragedy.

> Our fathers sinned, and are no more; and we bear their iniquities.   (Lam. 5:7)

It just doesn't seem fair—and it isn't. A drunken driver crosses the highway and wipes out an entire family. People are horrified and angry, repeatedly asking, Why? One family is healthy, their neighbors are sickly. The problem of unfair suffering has taxed the minds of countless philosophers and theologians. Yet here it is, in the Commandment, actually built into the order of the universe, as consistent as the law of gravity. People suffer for the sins of the fathers! It provoked the question asked of Jesus by his disciples: "Rabbi, who sinned, this man or his parents, that he was born blind?" (John 9:2).

Job makes an anguished cry against such injustice.

> "You say, 'God stores up their iniquity for their sons.' Let him recompense it to themselves, that they may know it. Let their own eyes see their destruction, and let them drink of the wrath of the Almighty. For what do they care for their houses after them, when the number of their months is cut off?"   (Job 21:19-21)

But Job's plea went unanswered: children continued to suffer for the iniquities of their great grandparents. The answer to this unfair dilemma still lay far into the future.

On the other hand, God promises "steadfast love" to those who love Him and keep his Commandments (Exodus 20:6). The reverse side of this coin of suffering is that God *blesses* the descendants of people who fear Him—whether those descendants are godly or not. Thousands of self-proclaimed atheists and occultists in America are enjoying lives that are blessed by God with good health, prosperity and relative contentment. In most cases we could trace their genealogies to locate godly ancestors. Of course, in the economy of God's world it will be the grandchildren of those atheists and occultists who will suffer most of the adverse consequences. And the cycle goes on. Revival will break out at some future date as the grandchildren call out to God in their distress, and the LORD—as faithful as ever—will hear their cry and respond in mercy. The 400 years of Israelite history covered by the Book of Judges provides the perfect biblical illustration of this cycle of the generations. It just seems that God's people cannot handle success; gradually He becomes "unnecessary."

The cyclical "law of the generations" is woven into the fabric of human history. The law of the generations surely must be a result of the curse of the Garden of Eden. Here in the Second Commandment God clearly enunciates this very real principle, a practical demonstration that "the spiritual" sooner or later controls "the physical."

But, what about those "innocent" victims in the third and fourth generations? Is there hope of breaking that tragic cycle during their lifetimes?

To leap ahead momentarily to the New Covenant,

> Christ redeemed us from the curse of the law, having become a curse for us . . . , that in Christ Jesus the blessing of Abraham might come upon the Gentiles, that we might receive the promise of the Spirit through faith.   (Gal. 3:13,14)

Because Jesus Christ redeemed us from the curse, and because we too have received God's blessing upon Abraham, and because we have received the Holy Spirit, we now can be freed from the curse of the generations "through faith." And so, that universal curse may be broken, broken for one believer at-a-time, through faith.

God intended this Second Commandment to be a *freeing* ordinance, setting his people free from polytheistic bondage. And it was freeing—but only for those who would obey. The pagan urges in the human heart, however, are so strong that many of the Israelites demanded a typical idolatrous orgy, as in the golden calf incident (Exodus 32).

Not only does he have difficulty handling *success*, but sin-prone man cannot handle *freedom* for a prolonged period. Many Israelites quickly gave up their freedom in the true Creator-God for the idolatrous bondage to which they had been accustomed.

Likewise, in America today we find countless people who would gladly give up their precious freedoms of democracy for the bondage of socialism or communism. These ideologies too are idolatry. Everybody needs a god to worship and manipulate. Those who reject the true God and Father of our Lord Jesus Christ are often found worshiping "Government"—in particular, a dictatorial type of government that promises material security while it takes away human liberties. They look to the national government, an idolatrous "god" they can manipulate, to provide the things for which they should look to the true God. This is "covetousness," a greed for material things, which the Apostle Paul calls idolatry (Eph. 5:5; Col. 3:5). It seems unbelievable, yet it's occurring in America today, even as in Moses' day. When people walk away from the Creator-God, they will always seek a false god to worship and manipulate.

The Second Commandment is quite rich in revelation. The LORD identified Himself as a "jealous God." This Hebrew word, *ganah*, means more than jealous; it means zealous, eager, passionate. He is a God with *feelings*! Since we were created in the image of God, we humans can well understand that word. No husband or wife wants to be treated as a "thing," something less than a person, by his or her mate. Worse yet, if one's spouse is involved in adultery, the injured mate's passions are deeply aroused; he or she is severely wounded and angry.

God is like that. Since He is Spirit, God is offended by man-made images or pictures being used to represent Him. He is further offended when his People go after other gods, which are only earthly demonic spirits serving in the kingdom of Satan. God thinks of this perversion as "adultery." An idolater among God's people can always eloquently and fervently justify his religious practices. But our God is a personal God, with strong feelings; yet so often his People act as if He can be manipulated or spurned. He is not merely a Creative Force—He is Somebody! God is personal! That's what is meant by the Hebrew word we usually translate as "jealous."

The Second Commandment began to be abused shortly after the Israelites entered the Promised Land. The Hebrews in the wilderness had been primarily a pastoral people, tending sheep, goats and some cattle. This remained the way of life for most of the southern tribes, where the land was drier, although some grain was grown in Judah (Bethlehem means "House of Bread"; see the Book of Ruth). The northern tribes, however, settled primarily in agricultural areas. Being unfamiliar with farming, the newly-located Israelites had to inquire of their pagan Canaanite neighbors about "agricultural science."

A Hebrew-Canaanite farming consultation might have gone like this: "You need to farm scientifically," instructed the Canaanite. "Planting must be done according to the direction of the Moon Goddess. She will guarantee fertility if you do it right. You also must do your part; if you want good crops you should get involved in the fertility rites in the village at planting time. You've got to demonstrate your own virility with the women here. You'll love it! And the more you participate in these sexual religious rites, the more fertile your fields and your animals will be. You see, your Hebrew God is a mountain God, a God of the wilderness. You're in a different culture now, and you've got to do it scientifically!"

Anyone can perceive how easily the Israelite farmers would have been entranced and excited by this "scientific" agriculture. Thus, the Second Commandment was violated repeatedly in farming areas. This apocryphal story describes the continuing problem faced by God's people through the centuries. It's called "scientism." Not science, but scientism.

Scientism is the word that describes any attempt by man to extend popular scientific theories into other areas of life, as religion. Scientism does indeed have strong religious qualities. We have seen how the prophets who called Israel to account for their idolatry became very unpopular with most of the citizenry. After all, the Hebrew farmers thought, we have to grow crops, and these prophets are interfering with the march of science! The farmers were confusing science with scientism.

Every few centuries such scientism attacks God's People with devastating force. Platonic philosophy severely undermined the faith of many Jews during the last three centuries before the birth of Jesus Christ. The scientistic (not scientific) effects of Platonism upon Judaism culminated in the writings of Philo Judaeus, a Jewish scholar who was writing in Egypt at the same time that Jesus of Nazareth was ministering in Galilee. Philo so diluted his Old Testament commentaries with Greek philosophy that his Jewish faith was hardly recognizable at times. Platonism had created the "science" of the day.

A century later another false teaching known as "gnosticism" began posing as superior science. Gnosticism was a clever combination of Iranian Zoroastrianism, Greek philosophy and Christianity. The early Christian Church was severely damaged by various gnostic heresies, because they seemed *so scientific.*

Later, in the Middle Ages, the ancient Greek Aristotle's teachings literally took over the Church's scholars. The Roman Catholic Church to this day is seriously hampered by the remnants of Aristotelian "science," a scientistic invasion which radically changed Catholic beliefs—for the worse—800 years ago. Later, Aristotle's writings even affected John Calvin's Reformed theology, as found in Congregationalism and Presbyterianism. Aristotelianism was accepted because it appeared to be scientific. Today we know better.

Our twentieth century problem in the Church is the direct philosophical descendant of Aristotelianism—modern rationalism, which is self-deluding. So-called "modern" man doesn't believe in miracles. God is becoming less and less necessary. The modern human mind is considered to be greater than the word of God. Rationalism is at the heart of liberalism (or, modernism) in the Church. The liberals in Christendom actually think they are "scientific" by not believing the whole Bible, by not accepting miracles, by espousing the very unscientific, pagan theory of evolution. This too is scientism, and such scientism has attacked the modern Church with devastating force, being taught authoritatively in most of our seminaries. It is much more logical, to the mind of fallen man, to worship the creation, rather than worship the Creator!

A modern example of what scientism can do to the Church involves Albert Einstein's theories. Early in this century Einstein proposed his Special Theory of Relativity; he later broadened his concepts to include what he called the General Theory of Relativity. Challenges came immediately from other scientists, so Einstein proposed a test involving an eclipse of the sun. Thus, in the year 1919, astronomers traveled to Africa to check his General Theory during a solar eclipse. The test showed Einstein to be correct, and upon his return to New York, Albert Einstein was given a ticker tape parade down Fifth Avenue.

But all was not well. A few—very few—other scientists checked Einstein's results carefully. And they found them to be faulty. What Einstein had claimed to be a demonstration of General Relativity was shown during the 1920's to be explainable by other means.

But it was too late. Most scientists had already joined the relativity bandwagon. Einstein had become a national hero. Scientific journals often refused to publish articles challenging his General Theory. Only today is the scientific world just beginning to re-examine Einstein's results from 1919.

This story is told only to demonstrate how currently-popular scientific theory affects the religion of the day. Today our world is being taught that not only is relativity true in science, it is true in other areas of life also. Liberal thinkers are confusing "relativity" with "relativism." To declare, as God did in the Decalogue, "You shall not. . . !" is considered by many liberal theologians today as "outmoded," "ancient," "unreal" in this modern world. Why? Because of a *scientistic* acceptance and unwarranted extension of Einstein's unproven Theory of General Relativity. All moral and ethical standards are now only *relative* to each person's viewpoint. The relativism of "situation ethics" has cursed the modern Church. This modern world perceives Christianity as still "evolving." Because of relativism's appeal, godliness in the American Church has suffered a severe decline in recent years. Even the Jewish Albert Einstein himself grieved deeply about this confusion.

So we see a tragic example of scientism's effects upon the Church today. The Ten Commandments are "out of style" for many theologians, pastors and laymen. This enormous problem all because of some faulty scientific deductions in 1919!

Actually, there are three partially-or totally-erroneous teachings that modern "rational" man has received gullibly, all of which have had profound negative effects upon the Church, as well as society in general. First came Charles Darwin's quite unscientific Theory of Evolution; second was psychiatrist Sigmund Freud's proposed structure of the human personality and his technique of psychoanalysis; and then followed Einstein's General Theory of Relativity. All three were accepted *without* rigorous scientific examination; today enormous scientific evidence is available to refute all three errors. But it's too late, the bandwagons have long been rolling.

Scientistic teachings are appealing, in spite of the fact that they will not stand up under careful investigation. Rebellious man accepts these concepts blindly, because the only alternative is obedience to the one, true Creator-God. Satan is "the god of this world," and he "has blinded the minds of the unbelievers" (2 Cor. 4:4). Whenever fallen man places his fallen intellect on the throne of his fallen life, Satan has an easy time. As long as the Thief rules this world, the Church will suffer from scientism.

In much the same way, scientism assailed the conquering Israelites as soon as they arrived in the Promised Land. Promiscuous pagan religion, posing as science, tempted God's Chosen People to violate the precious, freeing Second Commandment before they could even establish a history as a nation. As we have noted, this Second Commandment was indeed revolutionary. And it continued to be a very difficult ordinance to obey. Since God's blessings upon Israel were conditional upon their obedience to the Covenant, it would seem that the nation was early in jeopardy. Other Near Eastern nations had their own law codes—all of them quite religious, reflecting the traditions and morality of those nations—with qualities both good and evil. But the Creator-God demanded far more of Israel: "You shall be holy; for I the LORD your God am holy!" (Lev. 19:2).

The rest of the Commandments further reinforced this demand for holiness.

3. *You Shall Not Take the Name of the LORD Your God in Vain*.

"You shall not take the name of the LORD your God in vain; for the LORD will not hold him guiltless who takes his name in vain." (Exodus 20:7)

The Third Commandment is often misunderstood in modern America. Taking "the name of the LORD your God in vain" does not refer to profanity, as is usually assumed. The sin of using the LORD's name in profanity is more probably covered by Lev. 24:16:

> "He who blasphemes the name of the LORD shall be put to death; all the congregation shall stone him; the sojourner as well as the native, when he blasphemes the Name, shall be put to death."

Actually, we are not quite certain of the meaning of this Third Commandment; there are two possibilities.

First, we have already noted that, by possessing the image of the god, the idolater felt that he had some power over the god; the god could supposedly be cajoled or bribed into acting as its possessor requested. In Israel there were to be no images, but the Hebrews did possess God's own personal Name, Yahweh. No other people knew that Name. They also had the Ark of the Covenant. These "possessions" might be thought of as opportunities for idolatrous Israelites to try to "control" the LORD. The innate paganism in the hearts of many Israelites tempted them to think that their possessing the Name and the Ark would require the LORD to comply with their prayers.

But God's presence or blessing cannot be guaranteed, except by Himself. The Third Commandment, following directly after the Commandment against idolatry, has suggested to some scholars that it might thus be a further prohibition of idolatry.

God's very personal Name—The Name—Yahweh, was revealed to Moses at the Burning Bush. The Name reveals his personality and character. Yahweh is the Eternal One, the Almighty Creator, the Savior of Israel, the Living God.

He is over all the world He created, and his Name is to be reverenced. ("The LORD," in capital letters, is our English equivalent for his personal Name, Yahweh, in modern translations of the Bible). A wonderful scene occurred on Mt. Sinai when Moses climbed to meet God.

> And the LORD descended in the cloud and stood with him there, and proclaimed the name of the LORD. The LORD passed before him, and proclaimed, "The LORD, the LORD, a God merciful and gracious, slow to anger, and abounding in steadfast love and faithfulness, keeping steadfast love for thousands, forgiving iniquity and transgression and sin, but who will by no means clear the guilty, visiting the iniquity of the fathers upon the children and the children's children, to the third and the fourth generation."
>
> (Exodus 34:5-7)

The Name was indeed a very special treasure in Israel. Perhaps then this Third Commandment dealt with its misuse, the attempt to manipulate God by the knowledge of his personal Name. Whether or not this explains the Commandment, such attempts to coerce Him were rejected by the LORD, as the subsequent history of Israel demonstrated, again and again.

Most Bible students, however, feel that the Third Commandment refers to another prohibition, involving what is called the "oath of clearance." This is a judicial oath taken by an accused defendant in court. The Hebrew defendant could, if he wished, testify in his own trial, taking an oath of clearance: "If I have committed so-and-so crime, may God make me leprous, or strike me dead!" We have a model of this oath in Job 31. Job had been accused of sin by his "friends," so he takes the oath of clearance to prove his innocence. Job actually begins his oath with the key words, "I have made a covenant with my eyes . . . " (31:1). This chapter makes an interesting study, and the reader is urged to examine Job 31 before proceeding further. The probable intent of the Third Commandment is that if God's name is used in the oath of clearance and the defendant is lying, then he is taking the Name—Yahweh—in vain.

The Mosaic Covenant was designed by the Lord to provide also the *legal* framework for the Community of God. Israel was God's very own People, a People for his possession, and obedience to the Commandments would for ever maintain this unique relationship between Israel and their heavenly King.

The Lord didn't always distinguish, as humans do, between sacred and secular ordinances; all of human life is sacred to Him. Violation of either "religious" or "civil" ordinances threatened that relationship, indeed, threatened the very future of the entire nation. The court must be a place of honesty and justice; if the defendant in a trial violated the Third Commandment, the whole community's security was endangered. For then the God who protected them would be angered. Violation was to be punishable by death. Indeed, the breaking of any of the Ten Commandments but the final one was to be punishable by death: "So you shall purge the evil from the midst of you" (Deut. 13:5). We will note later the more specific expositions of these Commandments and the Punishment to be meted out to offenders.

4. *Remember the Sabbath Day, to Keep It Holy.*

"Remember the sabbath day, to keep it holy. Six days you shall labor, and do all your work; but the

seventh day is a sabbath to the LORD your God; in
it you shall not do any work, you, or your son,
or your daughter, your manservant, or your maidservant, or your cattle, or the sojourner who is
within your gates; for in six days the LORD made
heaven and earth, the sea, and all that is in them,
and rested the seventh day; therefore the LORD
blessed the sabbath day and hallowed it."

(Exodus 20:8-11)

Moses later repeated the Ten Commandments to a new,
young generation of Israelites, the generation that was to
inherit the Promised Land. Just before He died, Moses sum-
marized and restated the story of the previous 40 years. As
the retelling is recorded in Deuteronomy 5, an interesting
sentence is added to the sabbath stipulation, constituting
the only significant difference between the two versions of
the Decalogue.

"You shall remember that you were a servant in
the land of Egypt, and the LORD your God
brought you out thence with a mighty hand and
an outstretched arm; therefore, the LORD your
God commanded you to keep the sabbath day."

(Deut. 5:15)

According to Deuteronomy, the sabbath was to be observed,
among other reasons, as a memorial that Israel had been
slaves in Egypt. Further stipulations in Deuteronomy (15:15;
16:12; 24:18,22) reminded the Israelites of the same message: You shall not deny a day of rest to your slaves,
nor shall you oppress the foreigner, the widow or the
orphan! The additional sabbath stipulations in Deuteronomy

seem to approximate Exodus 22:21-24. Note that the Exodus passage is written in stronger language.

> "You shall not wrong a stranger or oppress him, for you were strangers in the land of Egypt. You shall not afflict any widow or orphan. If you do afflict them, and they cry out to me, I will surely hear their cry; and my wrath will burn, and I will kill you with the sword, and your wives shall become widows and your children fatherless."

Since the Hebrews perceived themselves to be God's Chosen People, it could logically have followed, to their thinking, that they would be justified in abusing foreigners who had settled in Israel temporarily or who might be traveling through their land. They could easily have assumed the Commandments to read, for example, "You shall not kill another Hebrew." "You shall not covet the property of another Hebrew." Certainly this narrow chauvinism was common in Israel. But the LORD demanded that they protect the alien too.

The Hebrew word for sabbath seems to have come from the root word for "rest." The sabbath had no *religious* significance in the beginning; the need for a seventh day of rest is simply another quality that God has built into the natural order of the universe. Very much like the "law of the generations," the sabbath is quite necessary for the world in which we live. God Himself gave the world the model for the sabbath when He rested on the seventh day of Creation Week. The Commandment was thus not merely for the Hebrews, but for all of mankind.

During the French Revolution of 1789 and its aftermath, the calendar was revised by the atheistic revolutionary government to eliminate all signs of biblical effect upon

French life. The seven-day week was changed to a ten-day week. It failed so miserably that, 13 years later, Napoleon rescinded the experiment, returning to the biblical pattern.

The Soviet Union attempted a similar revision in 1929. Beyond their usual incompetence and bungling, the Communist leadership was forced by the utter failure of this rebellious experiment to return within months to the biblical seven-day week. The Ten Commandments have a universal application, and peoples, nations and governments pay an ultimate price for ignoring them.

In Exodus 31:13 God narrowed the focus to make the sabbath a *sign* of the Mosaic Covenant.

> "You shall keep my sabbaths, for this is a sign between me and you throughout your generations, that you may know that I, the LORD, sanctify you."

Ezekiel later affirms the sabbath as a sign of the Mosaic Covenant.

> "Moreover I gave them my sabbaths, as a sign between me and them, that they might know that I the LORD sanctify them . . . I the LORD am your God; walk in my statutes, and be careful to observe my ordinances, and hallow my sabbaths that they may be a sign between me and you, that you may know that I the LORD am your God."
> (Ezekiel 20:12,19,20)

In the next verse the LORD showed his displeasure with his disobedient People.

"But the children rebelled against me; they did not walk in my statutes, and were not careful to observe my ordinances, by whose observance man shall live; they profaned my sabbaths."

(Ezekiel 20:21)

They profaned the sabbath by doing business on that day (the biblical sabbath is from sundown Friday to sundown Saturday). Yet that was apparently the lesser of their evils. Some Jewish slaveowners had been requiring their servants to work on the sabbath, giving them no day of rest. That is why the LORD had repeatedly reminded them in Deuteronomy to recall that *they* had once been slaves in Egypt.

Many centuries later the keeping of the sabbath became a *religious* matter, so overladen with rules and regulations that Jesus had to protest eloquently, "The sabbath was made for man, not man for the sabbath" (Mark 2:27). It was to be a day of freedom for *rest*, not a day for religious bondage. The religious lawyers in New Testament times would debate, for example, about how far a Jew was allowed by the Commandment to walk on the sabbath day. There was no unanimity about it, but the consensus seems to have been about one-third of a mile (1,000 paces), as Acts 1:12 notes that Olivet was "a sabbath day's journey" from Jerusalem. A longer walk on the sabbath would have been considered a sin by the rabbis. Modern orthodox Jews consider the religious keeping of the sabbath to be the primary outward distinction between themselves and the rest of humanity. However, many centuries had passed following the giving of the Ten Commandments before the sabbath became a day of religious observance.

There have been serious proposals by many Bible scholars that in their original form—the two stone tablets Moses brought down from Mt. Sinai—each of the Commandments was only one Hebrew word, preceded by the Hebrew negative, *lo*. They propose that the additional words were added to several of the Commandments when they were transcribed onto clay, parchment and papyrus in subsequent years. Hebrew words tend to be much richer in meaning than English words. They could say more with far fewer words. For example, Exodus 20:4, "You shall not make for yourself a graven image, or any likeness of anything that is in heaven above, or that is in the earth beneath, or that is in the water under the earth," contains only 16 Hebrew words, while 35 are required to translate this verse into good English. Note also the religious art of Judaism, where each Commandment is indeed pictured as two words.

So, perhaps the original Mosaic tables said something like this, in Hebrew only two words each:

1. I am Yahweh
2. No other gods
3. No name in vain
4. No sabbath work
5. No dishonor parents
6. No murder
7. No adultery
8. No steal
9. No false witness
10. No covet

Of course, we can never be certain of this, but it is a fascinating proposal.

We have noted the close parallels between the Mosaic Covenant and other Near Eastern covenants and law codes. Usually those pagan rules were conditional, as, "If you do that crime, this shall be your punishment." This is known as "casuistic," or "case" law. But the Ten Commandments were not conditional, they were "apodictic," direct Commandments, as, "You shall not. . . ! " Apodictic law was totally new to the people of the Near East. Again, much of the Mosaic Covenant was similar to what the Israelites were familiar with, yet there were also many radically-different features.

The Fourth Commandment, the weekly day of rest, was just as important as the other Commandments for maintaining the covenant relationship with God, for guaranteeing the stability of the nation, and for ensuring their permanent residence and prosperity in the Promised Land.

One ironic sidelight to the sabbath Commandment: God commanded a weekly day of not doing any work, neither "you, or your son, or your daughter, your manservant, or your maidservant, or your cattle, or the sojourner who is within your gates." Note that everybody got a day of rest— except the wife!

5. *Honor Your Father and Your Mother.*

"Honor your father and your mother, that your days may be long in the land which the LORD your God gives you."   (Exodus 20:12)

This Fifth Commandment was especially important to the future life of Israel; indeed, like several other Commandments, it is still vital to the survival of any people. If a nation's children are good to their elderly parents, God will be good to that nation: " . . . that your days may be long in the land which the LORD your God gives you." This Commandment expresses far more than the brief words indicate at first glance.

Many elaborations on the Ten Commandments follow immediately in Exodus 21 through 23, a catalog of ordinances known as the Covenant Code. We are reminded of the analogy of the Decalogue with the Constitution of the United States—brief and broad. The more detailed code of laws that derives from the Constitution may be likened to the expositions of the Ten Commandments that follow, from the remainder of Exodus as well as here and there throughout Leviticus, Numbers and Deuteronomy.

Thus, the Fifth Commandment could be written, "You shall not strike your father or your mother," as we see its elaboration in Exodus 21:15: "Whoever strikes his father or his mother shall be put to death." It could also be written, "You shall not curse your father or your mother," as we are told in Exodus 21:17: "Whoever curses his father or his mother shall be put to death." It could be written, "You shall not dishonor your mother or your father," for Lev. 19:3 says, "Every one of you shall revere his mother and his father." A further derivative of this Commandment should be added: "You shall not abandon your father or your mother in their old age" (see Jesus' bitter words in Mark 7:9-13).

Many primitive societies abandon their elderly to die, exposing them to the elements in the wilderness. Euthanasia is forbidden by this Commandment. Family solidarity was characteristic of Israelite life, and the Fifth Commandment is responsible. Thus Judaism and Christianity are both family oriented. The sign of a decaying society is the general attempt to shift the responsibility for caring for the elderly from the children to the state. God's word solemnly promises that a nation cannot last long when many of its citizens despise their elderly parents. That should be an ominous warning to America! Today, countless Americans are abandoning their helplessly senile parents near government-supported homes for the elderly, knowing that the parents will be found, and that the taxpayers will house and feed them until their deaths.

6. *You Shall Not Kill.*

"You shall not kill."   (Exodus 20:13)

The Sixth Commandment is more properly translated, "You shall not murder." Various forms of killing are distinguished by this Commandment. Human "murder" is the only act prohibited. Killing in warfare is not included, defensive killing (when one is being attacked) is not covered, nor is suicide included; capital punishment for violation of the Commandments is not only allowed, but commanded. Animal slaughter (whether for food, for sacrifice, or for clearing the land of dangerous beasts) is permissible; Albert Schweitzer's "reverence for life" (a form of Hinduism, in which all animal life is sacred) is utterly without biblical basis.

It is interesting to observe God's language as given through Moses. Again, we don't see the conditional quality, found in normal legal codes: "If you kill, you will be killed." The demonstrative nature of his words almost shouts, "You shall not commit murder!" We are reminded of the language used by Jesus Himself, the Son of God: "And they were astonished at his teaching, for he taught them as one who had authority, and not as the scribes" (Mark 1:22). The Ten Commandments are indeed unique.

7. *You Shall Not Commit Adultery.*

"You shall not commit adultery."
                                       (Exodus 20:14)

Again we see, as in the previous Commandment, a simple, two-Hebrew-word injunction, beginning with the Hebrew negative, "not." J. Edgar Park, in *The Interpreter's*

Bible*, tells of an English magazine that ran a competition in 1946 for the best new set of Ten Commandments. Entrants found special difficulty revising this Seventh Commandment. The editor finally admitted that Moses had done the best job: he was concrete, brief, and did not slip into the mere giving of advice.

Adultery is a word that refers only to sexual promiscuity by one who is married. Sexual intercourse involving the unmarried is called in the Bible "fornication." Fornication is covered by Exodus 22:16,17:

> "If a man seduces a virgin who is not betrothed, and lies with her, he shall give the marriage present for her, and make her his wife. If her father utterly refuses to give her to him, he shall pay money equivalent to the marriage present for virgins."

Of course, polygamous marriage was the accepted life style in 1500 B.C.; Moses himself had more than one wife. But, by the time of Jesus of Nazareth, monogamy had become the norm among the Jews. And fornication is universally condemned in the New Testament.

The Seventh Commandment was not intended to deal merely with the sexual aspect of sin. Since the Hebrew family was a social and economic *unit*, the man who seduced or forced another man's wife was committing, not only a sexual sin, but a crime against her husband, her family and the entire community. He was stealing someone who belonged to another man. The Mosaic Covenant was designed to ensure social and economic stability in Israel.

---

* New York and Nashville: Abingdon, 1952, Vol. I, p. 987.

This meant that human covenants also had to be meticulously observed. A violation of the solemn marriage covenant was to be treated as a major problem in the community; God took it quite seriously, and He expected his People to take it seriously.

If the Hebrews permitted adultery to go unpunished, the wrath of God could be expected. King David's adulterous sin was not merely sexual, nor was it committed against Bathsheba alone. The king's sin—apart from the subsequent murder—was a crime against her husband Uriah, as well as against their children, if there were any. Further, because he had offended God's Covenant stipulation, the LORD cursed the remainder of David's reign with warfare, scandal, rebellion and much national grief.

The same tragedy has occurred in modern America, where a flagrantly-adulterous President of the United States has left the nation a similar legacy of adultery, broken families, crime and great social unrest. A nation becomes like its leader. Unchecked violations of the Ten Commandments still exact a severe price upon any country.

In several of the prophetic books we find the LORD identifying Himself as Israel's *husband*. Thus, their repeated involvement with pagan gods He likened to adultery. Through Jeremiah, God spoke out against idolatry in colorful language.

"Have you seen what she did, that faithless one, Israel, how she went up on every high hill and under every green tree, and there played the harlot? And I thought, 'After she has done all this she will return to me'; but she did not return, and her false sister Judah saw it. She saw that for all the adulteries of that faithless one, Israel, I had sent her away with a decree of divorce; yet her false

> sister Judah did not fear, but she too went and
> played the harlot. Because harlotry was so light
> to her, she polluted the land, committing adultery
> with stone and tree."   (Jer. 3:6-9)

In spite of their repeated adulteries with foreign gods, the
LORD said He would forgive them and accept them back.
Hosea is the prophet of such "lovingkindness." Hosea's own
estranged wife, Gomer, had been a prostitute for so long that
no one wanted her anymore; she even had to sell herself
into slavery to get something to eat. Then God told the
prophet to take back his worn out, faithless wife. Hosea paid
the price to redeem his wife from slavery, and the LORD said
to Hosea, "I will do the same for faithless Israel if they will
only come back to me." Israel refused Hosea's prophetic message, and so the Northern Kingdom was destroyed within
30 years.

In the New Testament—in the Sermon on the Mount—
Jesus acknowledged the authority of the Seventh Commandment, but He increased its meaning to include "intent."

> "You have heard that it was said, 'You shall not
> commit adultery.' But I say to you that every
> one who looks at a woman lustfully has already
> committed adultery with her in his heart."
> (Matthew 5:27,28)

A misunderstanding of the word "lustfully" has caused
much unnecessary guilt and self-condemnation in countless
Christian men. The Commandment says, "You shall not
commit adultery." Jesus enlarged upon it in this manner:
"You shall not even *plot* to commit adultery." Men are
naturally drawn to admire attractive women, but this is not
what Jesus was referring to. He was alluding rather to the

man who is scheming to seduce another's man's wife; although the man has not actually committed the overt act of adultery, Jesus said he has done it in his heart. Much less guilt would have been incurred among Christian men if the Church had been blessed with teaching based upon proper biblical exegesis. The *intent* is the key, according to the New Testament.

8. *You Shall Not Steal.*

"You shall not steal."   (Exodus 20:15)

This prohibition has nothing whatsoever to do with stealing property; that crime is covered by the Tenth Commandment. The Eighth Commandment deals with the stealing of *people* for the purpose of making them slaves or selling them into slavery. It refers to persons, not property. The kidnapping and selling of Joseph by his older brothers is such an example.

> "Whoever steals a man, whether he sells him or
> is found in possession of him, shall be put to
> death."   (Exodus 21:16)

Here we find the exposition of the Eighth Commandment. The reader will note that the punishment for violation is death. The stealing of personal property was never punishable by death in Israel, only the stealing of a person. Widows, orphans and aliens were "fair game" for unscrupulous Israelites; this prohibition was designed to defend the defenseless.

During the Crusades of the Middle Ages, which were organized to wrest the Holy Land from the grip of its Moslem conquerors, one such effort was known as the Children's Crusade. In the summer of the year 1212 much religious zeal was generated among the boys of southern France, thousands of whom marched to the port of Marseilles, planning to sail to win the Holy Land "with love." Slavetrading sea captains offered to take the youthful Crusaders to Palestine at no cost, but enticed them on board only to sell them into slavery in Moslem Egypt. This was a gross violation of the Eighth Commandment.

The detailed expositions of the Ten Commandments are partially catalogued below. Most of the elaborations are found immediately following the Decalogue, in the Covenant Code (Exodus 21-23). Further elaborations are found later in Exodus, in Leviticus, Numbers and Deuteronomy. Each Commandment is listed by verse in the left-hand column, and many of the related ordinances are listed in the column on the right. An asterisk is found beside a passage that includes the death penalty for violation.

Exodus 20	*Exposition*
1) verse 2	Exodus 20:22; Lev. 24:16*
2) verses 3-6	Exodus 20:23; 22:18*; 22:20*; 23:13; Lev. 19:4; 24:16*; Deut. 4:15-19
3) verse 7	Exodus 22:11; Lev. 19:12; Num. 15:30,31*
4) verses 8-11	Exodus 23:12; 31:13-17*; 35:2,3*; Lev. 19:3
5) verse 12	Exodus 21:15*; 21:17*; Lev. 19:3; 20:9*
6) verse 13	Exodus 21:12-14*; Lev. 24:17*
7) verse 14	Lev. 20:10*; Deut. 22:22*
8) verse 15	Exodus 21:16*; Deut. 24:7*
9) verse 16	Exodus 23:1-3; Deut. 19:15-21*
10) verse 17	Exodus 22:1-15

Note that a violation of any Commandment except the Tenth was punishable by death. The LORD demanded a holy people!

> "Your eye shall not pity; it shall be life for life, eye for eye, tooth for tooth, hand for hand, foot for foot." (Deut. 19:21)

9. *You Shall Not Bear False Witness Against Your Neighbor.*

> "You shall not bear false witness against your neighbor." (Exodus 20:16)

Whereas the Third Commandment probably referred to the *accused* perjuring himself in court, this Ninth Commandment dealt with the *witness* in a trial.

The Babylonian law code of King Hammurabi, dating only slightly earlier than Moses, stated that the bearer of false witness, if discovered in his perjury, was to be sentenced to the punishment expected to be meted out to the one he had falsely accused. So it was in Israel.

> "If a malicious witness rises against any man to accuse him of wrongdoing, then both parties to the dispute shall appear before the LORD, before the priests and the judges who are in office in those days; the judges shall inquire diligently, and if the witness is a false witness and has accused his brother falsely, then you shall do to him as he had meant to do to his brother; so you shall purge the evil from the midst of you. And the rest shall hear, and fear, and shall never again commit any such evil among you." (Deut. 19:16-20)

This Commandment against false witness could be considered the basis for the integrity of Israel's legal system. If witnesses are allowed to testify falsely without fear of severe punishment, any nation's legal system is in jeopardy. The integrity of Israel's courts was essential to the whole community, as well as to the community's relationship to God.

> "On the evidence of two witnesses or of three
> witnesses he that is to die shall be put to death;
> a person shall not be put to death on the evidence
> of one witness." (Deut. 17:6)

English common law, the basis for our American system of jurisprudence, allows a defendant to be convicted—even sentenced to death—on the basis of only one witness's testimony, or even mere circumstantial evidence. But Israelite law would rather allow the guilty to escape justice than an innocent man be put to death. Israel's Covenant Code would not permit such an opportunity for a single malicious accuser.

Again, as in the Third Commandment, the Name—Yahweh—could not be profaned, in a false oath sworn by a witness. The Name was too precious, too holy, and a false witness must be executed promptly upon being discovered.

We must be careful to note that the Ninth Commandment refers *only* to lying in court trials, not ordinary lying in business, for example. In fact, in Semitic cultures to this day, lying in a business deal is an art, not a sin. We must beware of forcing our Christian ethics upon people who are not Christian.

The most notable Old Testament violation of the Ninth Commandment was the incident involving Naboth's vineyard. In 1 Kings 21 King Ahab of Israel desired to own the land adjoining his palace in Jezreel, but it was a vineyard belonging to Naboth, who refused to sell it. Ahab's wife, the infamous Queen Jezebel, wrote letters to the elders of Jezreel, instructing them to hale Naboth into court. To give the pretense of legality, they were to hire "two base fellows" to charge Naboth with the crime of blasphemy against God and the king. Then, said Jezebel, take him out and stone him. Notice that the evil queen was careful to insist upon *two* accusers, as the scripture says.

> "A single witness shall not prevail against a man
> for any crime or for any wrong in connection with
> any offense that he has committed; only on the
> evidence of two witnesses, or of three witnesses,
> shall a charge be sustained."   (Deut. 19:15)

Naboth was convicted by a deliberate, royal perversion of the Ninth Commandment. For this heinous crime God declared through Elijah the prophet the most severe punishment: the dogs of Jezreel would lick up King Ahab's blood, and they did (1 Kings 22:38). Further, the dogs of Jezreel would eat the dead body of Queen Jezebel, and they did (2 Kings 9:30-37). This demonstrates again how seriously God views violations of the Commandments.

Jesus Himself was convicted in a kangaroo court by the chief priests and some elders and scribes following their attempted violation of the Ninth Commandment, but the chief priests were unable to get two false witnesses to give exactly the same testimony.

> Now the chief priests and the whole council
> sought testimony against Jesus to put him to death;
> but they found none. For many bore false witness
> against him, and their witness did not agree. And

> some stood up and bore false witness against him,
> saying, "We heard him say, 'I will destroy this
> temple that is made with hands, and in three days
> I will build another, not made with hands.' "
> (Mark 14:55-58).

According to Matthew 26:60, "At last two came forward . . . " and agreed. The chief priests, pretending, like Jezebel, to be very careful to observe proper Ninth Commandment justice, did not condemn Jesus until He finally claimed to be the Messiah (Mark 14:61-64).

For this mockery of obedience to the Covenant, God allowed the Jewish nation to be destroyed 40 years later by the Romans, and the remnant scattered or sold into slavery. How seriously God views the perversion of justice!

10. *You Shall Not Covet.*

> "You shall not covet your neighbor's house; you
> shall not covet your neighbor's wife, or his manservant, or his maidservant, or his ox, or his ass,
> or anything that is your neighbor's."
> (Exodus 20:17)

In modern English this final Commandment sounds as if it deals with intent. Actually, however, the enforcement of this stipulation could occur in court only if a man had been discovered in possession of incriminating evidence. Then and only then could the accused's intentions become important. Intent of course might be important in modern American jurisprudence also, even as in ancient Israel. Once physical evidence of a crime is made available, that is when the intent or motivation, becomes important—but only if material evidence of the theft is found.

Jesus is the One who added intent to the Commandments. The Tenth Commandment speaks to the act of stealing itself, not to the plotting to steal; intent to steal is hardly possible for a court to ascertain.

There are various Old Testament formulas for restitution of stolen goods.

> "If a man steals an ox or a sheep, and kills it or sells it, he shall pay five oxen for an ox, and four sheep for a sheep . . . He shall make restitution; if he has nothing, then he shall be sold for his theft. If the stolen beast is found alive in his possession, whether it is an ox or an ass or a sheep, he shall pay double."   (Exodus 22:1,3,4)

Zacchaeus, the chief tax collector of Jericho, promised to repay "fourfold" anything he had obtained illegally (Luke 19:1-10). Obviously Zacchaeus was thinking of this scripture in Exodus. See also King David's statement in 2 Samuel 12:6. Fourfold restitution—when enforced—was a strong deterrent to theft. And if the thief couldn't repay, he was to be sold into slavery, which was an even stronger deterrent.

The elders of the villages of Israel held court "in the gate." The most comfortable place in the hot Near Eastern summer was the shade of the tunnel—the gate—through the city wall. There in the cool shadows, the elders listened to disputes and dispensed justice. The Book of Proverbs is laden with counsel conforming to the Mosaic Covenant, much of which must certainly have been developed through the centuries "in the gate." God considered the village gates to be the most important places in all of Israel. If justice was perverted, if bribes were taken, if friendship or kinship became a factor in the decisions, the whole fabric of

Israelite society was threatened and the Covenant relationship with God was broken. Justice was critically important.

> "Hear the cases between your brethren, and judge righteously between a man and his brother or the alien that is with him. You shall not be partial in judgment; you shall hear the small and the great alike; you shall not be afraid of the face of man, for the judgment is God's." (Deut. 1:16,17)

In a nation where the fear of God was strong, the apodictic, demonstrative quality of the Commandment surely had its effect: The LORD said, "You shall not. . . !'' That type of statement alone should have been a deterrent to crime.

We noted earlier the great similarity between the Hittite suzerainty covenants and the Mosaic Covenant. Violation of a Hittite covenant called for retribution by the gods; no human retaliation was even mentioned. Yet, we know that if a vassal ruler rebelled, the Hittite suzerain (the superior party to the covenant) would hardly wait on the gods, but rather would anticipate wreaking very earthly vengeance against his rebellious subject quite promptly. In the Decalogue, God expected the Israelite community to do the punishing of Covenant violators— also quite promptly. Otherwise, He might destroy the whole nation.

The Ten Commandments have had dramatic consequences upon legal codes and cultures wherever the Bible has been widely available. The U.S. Supreme Court Building has the Decalogue prominently displayed on its walls. English common law has been infused by the Commandments and many of its Old Testament derivatives. William Blackstone, English history's most famous lawyer, deliberately modelled his work after Old Testament law. Thus we may note the success, historically, of English common law wherever it has been adopted across the earth.

Many countries—far beyond ancient Israel—have realized the universal genius and validity of the Ten Commandments. God knows all too well that the close-knit family and the integrity of the judicial system are both essential to the life of a nation, so He wove together in the Covenant the basic rules of faith and of ethics. Religious-ethical norms, according to the LORD, are far more important to a nation than political-economic norms. Would that the American people could perceive that truth as did so many of our country's founders!

Many of the founding fathers of the United States of America had a distinct sense of God's calling, of being a people in covenant with God. American education was then largely Presbyterian/Congregational, both based upon the Calvinist Reformed tradition. Having sat through countless Congregational, Reformed or Presbyterian sermons, a number of these early American statesmen were heavily influenced by the idea of the Covenant-community in ancient Israel. This explains the strong Old Testament flavor of the U. S. Constitution and some of the first state constitutions. Our early American leaders could feel a kinship with the People to whom God would say,

> "Now therefore, if you will obey my voice and keep my covenant, you shall be my own possession among all peoples; for all the earth is mine, and you shall be to me a kingdom of priests and a holy nation."   (Exodus 19:5,6)

Not merely the descendants of Aaron, but all of God's People were to be "priests" before God. Not only the Levites, who were specifically set apart to praise the LORD, but the whole nation was to praise Him.

> "I made the whole house of Israel and the whole house of Judah cling to me, says the LORD, that they might be for me a people, a name, a praise, and a glory."   (Jer. 13:11)

Israel was

> " . . . my chosen people, the people whom I formed for myself that they might declare my praise."   (Isa. 43:21)

Israel was to be "a kingdom of priests and a holy nation." They were a People for God's own possession, especially blessed by the holy God, and especially expected to be holy by the God who blessed them. Throughout the centuries Israel and, later, the Divided Kingdoms also, still considered themselves the "holy nation" among their neighbors—in spite of their misbehavior.

The Broken Covenant

Israel saw, during the conquest of the Promised Land, the "terrible things" God accomplished for his part of the Mosaic Covenant. Walls collapsed, stones fell from the sky, other peoples trembled with fear before the Hebrew conquerors.

> And Israel served the LORD all the days of Joshua, and all the days of the elders who outlived Joshua

> and had known all the work which the LORD did
> for Israel.   (Joshua 24:31)

But Israel's part in the Covenant—keeping the Commandments—was too difficult for an entire nation. Violation became widespread, although significant numbers continued to hold a "fear of the Lord."

What happens when a covenant is broken? There are three possible responses: one, immediate retribution; two, delayed retribution; and three, forgiveness. The injured party to the covenant has the options, not the one who broke the covenant. The covenant-breaker is at the mercy of the other party. In the case of the Mosaic Covenant, God said, "You shall purge the evil from the midst of you" (Deut. 19:19). But increasingly Israel failed to punish covenant-breakers, primarily because it is quite difficult to convict influential people in any society. Deut. 1:17 spoke to this problem.

> "You shall not be partial in judgment; you shall
> hear the small and the great alike; you shall not
> be afraid of the face of man, for the judgment is
> God's."

So God had to make repeated decisions concerning the violations. We find that at different times the LORD followed each of the three courses. Achan suffered immediate punishment for his sin in Joshua 7; the Kingdom of Judah suffered delayed (by a century) punishment for the sins of the evil King Manasseh; and King David received forgiveness for having broken the Sixth and Seventh Commandments (involving Bathsheba and Uriah) in 2 Samuel 12:13.

> David said to Nathan, "I have sinned against the
> LORD." And Nathan said to David, "The LORD also
> has put away your sin; you shall not die."

The course to be followed is always at God's discretion. Only
the One who has been offended may repair the broken
Covenant.

Finally, after repairing so many times, God declared
through Jeremiah that, first, He was going to execute judgment, and, second, He would one day make a "new
covenant,"

> " . . . not like the covenant which I made with
> their fathers when I took them by the hand to
> bring them out of the land of Egypt, my covenant
> which they broke, though I was their husband,
> says the LORD."   (Jer. 31:31,32)

But this New Covenant was still many centuries from the
days of Achan, David and Manasseh.

Since the LORD was a God of war, Israel should not have
needed any other king. The LORD was King of kings! For
400 difficult years God held off Israel's natural desire for
an earthly king who would fight their battles for them. They
wanted a strong central government; their loose confeder-
acy was literally falling apart, as we see in the Book of Judges.
The prophet Samuel made a last-ditch effort to maintain this
full Covenant relationship with the LORD, but it was a lost
cause.

> Then all the elders of Israel gathered together and
> came to Samuel at Ramah, and said to him,
> "Behold, you are old and your sons do not walk
> in your ways; now appoint for us a king to

govern us like all the nations." But the thing displeased Samuel when they said, "Give us a king to govern us." And Samuel prayed to the LORD.

And the LORD said to Samuel, "Hearken to the voice of the people in all that they say to you; for they have not rejected you, but they have rejected me from being king over them. According to all the deeds which they have done to me, from the day I brought them up out of Egypt even to this day, forsaking me and serving other gods, so they are also doing to you. Now then, hearken to their voice; only, you shall solemnly warn them, and show them the ways of the king who shall reign over them."   (1 Samuel 8:4-9)

So Samuel reluctantly anointed the man God pointed out to him, Saul. This passage from 1 Samuel describes the ultimate end of the union of Israel with the LORD as their King.

Because people are accustomed to bilateral covenants, God had made such a covenant with Israel at Mt. Sinai. Most humans feel uncomfortable unless they can do this for that, give something in exchange for something else. Man does not like the feeling of "owing" another person, even owing God. Mark Twain said that the only difference between a man and a dog is that a dog won't bite your hand when you feed him. By righteous living and proper sacrifices, Israel could have walked comfortably and happily before God. But natural man is still an idolater at heart, desirous of manipulating even Almighty God. So the Mosaic Covenant enjoyed a spotty record of success, even in its best times. And, of course, the LORD surely knew from the beginning the failures that would occur in the years to come.

> And the LORD said to Moses, "Behold, you are
> about to sleep with your fathers; then this peo-
> ple will rise and play the harlot after the strange
> gods of the land, where they go to be among them,
> and they will forsake me and break my covenant
> which I have made with them."   (Deut. 31:16)

Renewals of the Mosaic Covenant

Amid the numerous national violations of their vows,
God's People, always under the leadership of one man,
renewed the Mosaic Covenant on various occasions during
Old Testament history. Of course, a biblical covenant could
only be initiated by the Superior Party, God Himself. So the
following seven covenants, initiated by man, must be
considered merely to be periodic human revivals of the same
Mosaic Covenant.

First, Moses himself renewed the bilateral Covenant 39
years after the Covenant was initially established at Sinai.
This was in preparation for Moses' death and Israel's enter-
ing the Promised Land (Deut. 5).

Second, Joshua, the successor to Moses, renewed the
Mosaic Covenant before his death (Joshua 23:16; 24:25).

Third, many centuries later King Asa of Judah, the great
grandson of Solomon, proclaimed a renewal of the Covenant (2 Chron. 15:12). He was so zealous for the LORD that

> Even Maacah, his mother, King Asa removed from
> being queen mother because she had made an
> abominable image for Asherah. Asa cut down her
> image, crushed it, and burned it at the brook
> Kidron.   (2 Chron. 15:16.)

Fourth, four generations of royalty later, Jehoiada the high priest instigated a revolt against Queen Athaliah, the evil daughter of Jezebel (2 Kings 11:17). After Athaliah had been assassinated, Jehoiada led Judah in a national renewal of the Mosaic Covenant once more, because the People had been seduced into idolatry by Athaliah.

Fifth, Hezekiah, the courageous, reforming king of Judah, initiated a renewal of the Covenant (2 Chron. 29:10). He totally reversed the pagan policies of his evil father Ahaz, reopening the Temple which King Ahaz had padlocked.

Sixth, Hezekiah's great grandson, King Josiah, renewed the Mosaic Covenant in dramatic fashion (2 Kings 23:3), doing his best to eradicate completely all evidence of idolatry from the land. The fourth, fifth and sixth renewals of the Covenant all followed particularly evil rulers. But the earlier, evil reign of Josiah's grandfather, King Manasseh, was one too many, for God had already proclaimed Judah's ultimate doom, scheduled by the LORD to occur twenty years after Josiah's death (2 Kings 23:21-27).

Thus the Babylonians under King Nebuchadnezzar destroyed the exquisite Temple of Solomon, which had stood gloriously for more than 350 years. Nebuchadnezzar marched most of Jerusalem's survivors, in chains, hundreds of miles north and east to Babylon. Too many times God's Chosen People had refused to live by the Covenant to which their fathers had agreed at the foot of Mt. Sinai. The LORD felt He had to submit them to the ultimate chastening.

Fifty years later some of the Jews began to straggle back from Babylon to the Land sworn to them by the God of the Unbreakable Promise. Other groups followed through the next century, although the last of the Jews finally returned from the land of Babylon as recently as this present generation, when many were cruelly driven out by the Iraqis.

Seventh, and finally, during the fifth century B.C., Ezra the high priest and Nehemiah the governor collaborated to renew the Mosaic Covenant one more time (Nehemiah 9:38; 10:29). The idolatrous spirit in the Jewish hearts had been broken. Outward observances, as circumcision, dietary laws and the keeping of the sabbath, distinguished the Jews more than ever from their neighbors.

Within several centuries a belief arose among some Jewish religious teachers that if all of Israel would just "keep the Law" for only one day, the LORD would be obligated to establish his eternal kingdom. "Law" was replacing "Covenant." And Jerusalem languished under successive Persian, Greek, Egyptian, Syrian and Roman rules. The brief, hundred-year period of Jewish independence from 166 B.C. to 63 B.C. was characterized by several Jewish rulers who were sometimes more cruel than their foreign oppressors had been. 1500 fitful years of alternating obedience to and violation of the Mosaic Covenant had passed when Jesus of Nazareth began his ministry in Galilee.

The bilateral Covenant would have to be judged as a failure.

II

The Unilateral Covenants

Of the five Old Testament covenants between God and man, the Covenant with Moses is the only one that is bilateral. The Mosaic Covenant has also received most of the publicity, both within and without the Bible. But the 39 books (the Old Testament) cannot be understood until the remaining covenants have also been studied. Now we will examine the other four.

The Noahic Covenant

The first Covenant between God and man appears, not in the Garden of Eden, but many centuries later, in Genesis 9. First, God anticipated this Covenant with Noah in Gen. 6:17,18, before the Flood.

> "For behold, I will bring a flood of waters upon
> the earth. . . ; everything that is on the earth shall
> die. But I will establish my covenant with you."

A year after the rain began to fall, Noah finally crawled out of the Ark onto dry ground and quickly made a sacrifice to God.

Then Noah built an altar to the LORD, and took of every clean animal and of every clean bird, and offered burnt offerings on the altar. And when the LORD smelled the pleasing odor, the LORD said in his heart, "I will never again curse the ground because of man, for the imagination of man's heart is evil from his youth; neither will I ever again destroy every living creature as I have done."
(Gen. 8:20,21)

Blood was shed on that altar, and God chose this moment to confirm the Covenant with Noah (and all his descendants), the *first* of the biblical covenants. This was his Covenant with the whole human race.

"Behold, I establish my covenant with you and your descendants after you, and with every living creature that is with you, the birds, the cattle, and every beast of the earth with you, as many as came out of the ark. I establish my covenant with you, that never again shall all flesh be cut off by the waters of a flood, and never again shall there be a flood to destroy the earth."
(Gen. 9:9-11)

Covenants have signs. The deed to a home, for example, is the sign of a covenant between seller and buyer. The *sabbath* was the sign of the Mosaic Covenant.

"Say to the people of Israel, 'You shall keep my sabbaths, for this is a sign between me and you throughout your generations.' "   (Exodus 31:13)

So the Noahic Covenant had a sign also.

> And God said, "This is the sign of the cove-
> nant which I make between me and you and
> every living creature that is with you, for all
> future generations: I set my bow in the cloud,
> and it shall be a sign of the covenant between
> me and the earth. When I bring clouds over the
> earth and the bow is seen in the clouds, I will
> remember my covenant which is between me
> and you and every living creature of all flesh;
> and the waters shall never again become a flood
> to destroy all flesh. When the bow is in the clouds,
> I will look upon it and remember the everlasting
> covenant between God and every living creature
> of all flesh that is upon the earth."
>
> (Gen. 9:12-16)

The distinctive difference between the Noahic Covenant
and the Mosaic Covenant is that the bilateral, conditional
quality of the Mosaic Covenant is lacking. God did not say
to Noah, "If you and your descendants behave yourselves,
I will never again destroy the earth by water." He simply
made an unconditional, unilateral commitment in which the
full burden of fulfillment remained upon Himself. Only
God—the Superior Party—was bound by this pledge. We
could assume that such a covenant was unheard of in human
religions and cultures. As someone said years ago, Noah had
no more responsibility for fulfilling any aspect of the
Covenant than he had the responsibility for placing the rain-
bow in the sky.

So, in Genesis 9 we find not only the first biblical Covenant, but also the Covenant that established the unilateral precedent.

The Abrahamic Covenant

Ten generations after Noah, but still several hundred years before Moses, God singled out a man named Abram.

> Now the LORD said to Abram, "Go from your country and your kindred and your father's house to the land that I will show you. And I will make of you a great nation, and I will bless you, and make your name great, so that you will be a blessing. I will bless those who bless you, and him who curses you I will curse; and by you all the families of the earth shall bless themselves."
>
> (Gen. 12:1-3)

Abram was obedient to the word of the LORD; he left Haran and went to Canaan. Again God spoke to Abram, in a vision. Abram took the opportunity to question the LORD about his wife's childlessness.

> And Abram said, "Behold, thou hast given me no offspring; and a slave born in my house will be my heir." And behold, the word of the LORD came to him, "This man shall not be your heir; your own son shall be your heir." And he brought him outside and said, "Look toward heaven, and number the stars, if you are able to number them."

> Then he said to him, "So shall your descendants
> be." And he believed the Lord; and he reckoned
> it to him as righteousness.   (Gen. 15:3-6)

Abram was past 75 years of age when God made that
promise. The Lord was delighted that Abram would believe
so astonishing a pledge. God especially appreciates those
who have faith in his sometimes-incredible promises: "And
he reckoned it to him as righteousness." Then the Lord
said,

> "I am the Lord who brought you from Ur of the
> Chaldeans, to give you this land to possess."
>   (Gen. 15:7)

Abram had believed God, but he was old and childless, and
all these delightful promises must have bewildered him. He
looked around and saw that the land was fully settled by
Amorites, Canaanites and others. It all seemed impossible.
So Abram asked, "O Lord God, how am I to know that I
shall possess it?" (Gen. 15:8).

The Lord responded to Abram with a command that
would have been quite familiar in the Near Eastern world
of 2000 B.C.

> He said to him, "Bring me a heifer three years old,
> a she-goat three years old, a ram three years old,
> a turtledove, and a young pigeon." And he brought
> him all these, cut them in two, and laid each half
> over against the other; but he did not cut the birds
> in two.   (Gen. 15:9,10)

This type of sacrifice was common to the ancient Hebrews
and their neighbors. In the Hittite suzerainty covenants, as

well as other similar treaties and agreements, the *inferior* of the two parties, the puppet ruler who was submitting to the superior Hittite suzerain, was required to seal the covenant with his Hittite lord by taking his oath while *passing between the pieces of the split animals*. As he walked between the bloodied halves, the vassal ruler would say, "May the gods do so to me, and more also, if I do not live up to the terms of this covenant!"

Now the reader is urged to turn in the Bible to Jeremiah 34:8 and read to the end of the chapter. Please interrupt your reading of this book to examine that scripture, for it will explain how such a covenant is made.

To explain the story from Jeremiah 34, Nebuchadnezzar, the Babylonian king, was besieging Jerusalem in 588 B.C. In their great fear, the priests, the nobles and the rich made a covenant before the LORD that they would obey the Mosaic Covenant stipulation which commanded that all Hebrew slaves be freed by their masters each seventh year, the year of release.

> "When you buy a Hebrew slave, he shall serve six
> years, and in the seventh he shall go out free, for
> nothing."   (Exodus 21:2)

Until that time, many influential Jerusalemites had been ignoring this obligation by keeping their slaves indefinitely. But with Jerusalem in danger of falling to the Babylonian army, the nobles suddenly "got religion." They split a calf in the traditional manner and all of them walked between the halves, saying, "May the LORD do so to me, and more also, if I do not keep the conditions of this covenant!" And they released the slaves.

Suddenly Pharaoh of Egypt made a move toward the Babylonians with his army. Nebuchadnezzar had to lift the siege of Jerusalem and prepare to fight the Egyptians to the west. When the priests, the wealthy and the nobility of Jerusalem saw that Nebuchadnezzar had lifted the siege, they assumed that the LORD had delivered the city. Ignoring their solemn covenant, they promptly celebrated the deliverance by seizing their former slaves and putting them back into bondage again. But, before the two armies could engage in battle, the timid Pharaoh hurriedly retreated to the temporary safety of Egypt.

The LORD was deeply angered. Such hypocritical people actually think He is a distant, unhearing, unseeing God. So the LORD instructed Jeremiah to tell these faithless slaveowners that He would indeed do to them as they had sworn.

> "Their dead bodies shall be food for the birds of the air and the beasts of the earth. And Zedekiah king of Judah, and his princes I will give into the hand of their enemies and into the hand of those who seek their lives, into the hand of the army of the king of Babylon which has withdrawn from you. Behold, I will command, says the LORD, and will bring them back to this city; and they will fight against it, and take it, and burn it with fire. I will make the cities of Judah a desolation without inhabitant."
>
> (Jer. 34:20-22)

This story demonstrates how casually the leadership of Judah in 588 B.C. took the Mosaic Covenant. They didn't really believe that the living God meant exactly what

He said. Zephaniah had earlier prophesied harshly of that same generation,

> " . . . those who say in their hearts, 'The Lord will not do good, nor will he do ill.' " (Zeph. 1:12)

"May the LORD do so to me, and more also!" developed into the language of a casual oath, as we note how often those words appeared later in the Old Testament, usually when the speaker was angry.

The concept of cutting and passing between the two halves of the sacrificial animals actually gave the institution of covenant-making its name. Whenever our English Old Testament speaks of "making a covenant," the original Hebrew word is "cutting"—"cutting a covenant." Quoting the LORD in his anger, Jeremiah says,

> "And the men who transgressed my covenant and did not keep the terms of the covenant which they *made* before me, I will make like the calf which they cut in two and passed between its parts . . . "
>
> (Jer. 34:18)

A *literal* translation from the Hebrew reads as follows.

> "And I will give the men who transgressed my covenant, who did not establish the words of the covenant which they *cut* before me—the calf which they cut in two and passed between its pieces . . . "

So the expression, "to cut a covenant," became, through the ancient centuries, "to make a covenant." We are reminded of the modern Americanism, "to cut a deal."

But back to Abram in Genesis 15. After Abram split and separated the halves of the animals that he was sacrificing at the LORD's command, there occurred one of the most awesome experiences recorded in the Bible.

> As the sun was going down, a deep sleep fell on Abram; and lo, a dread and great darkness fell upon him . . . When the sun had gone down and it was dark, behold, a smoking fire pot and a flaming torch passed between these pieces. On that day the LORD made a covenant with Abram, saying, "To your descendants I give this land, from the river of Egypt to the great river, the river Euphrates."
>
> (Gen. 15:12,17,18)

In a spectacular display of condescension, the Superior Party humbled Himself to take on the role of the inferior party to the Covenant. *God Himself passed between the halves of the sacrifice!*

The expression, "a smoking fire pot and a flaming torch" is apparently a grammatical form often used in biblical Hebrew called "hendiadys" (hen-dye'-a-dis). One phrase modifies the other in hendiadys, so that there was actually described a single, spectacular fire that passed between the severed animals. We are reminded of the burning bush on Mt. Sinai (Exodus 3:2), as well as the blazing fire in which God later descended upon Mt. Sinai during a fearsome display (Exodus 19:18). He also led Israel through the wilderness by a pillar of fire. Fire is often associated with the throne of God in the Bible (Ezekiel 1:27; Daniel 7:9; Rev. 4:5).

We may be sure that Abram never forgot that incredible evening. Later generations of Hebrews could not forget it either. The Abrahamic Covenant is the most important Covenant in the Old Testament! More important than the Mosaic Covenant that so dominates the majority of scripture! Later we will discover why it is so vital.

Let's examine together *all* of God's promises to Abram.

> "And I will make of you a great nation, and I will bless you, and make your name great, so that you will be a blessing. I will bless those who bless you, and him who curses you I will curse; and by you all the families of the earth shall bless themselves. . . . To your descendants I will give this land."
>
> (Gen. 12:2,3,7)

> The LORD said to Abram . . . "Lift up your eyes, and look from the place where you are, northward and southward and eastward and westward; for all the land which you see I will give to you and to your descendants for ever. I will make your descendants as the dust of the earth; so that if one can count the dust of the earth, your descendants also can be counted. Arise, walk through the length and the breadth of the land, for I will give it to you."
>
> (Gen. 13:14-17)

> After these things the word of the LORD came to Abram in a vision, "Fear not, Abram, I am your shield; your reward shall be very great . . . This man shall not be your heir; your own son shall be your heir." And he brought him

outside and said, "Look toward heaven, and number the stars, if you are able to number them." Then he said to him, "So shall your descendants be." . . . And he said to him, "I am the LORD who brought you from Ur of the Chaldeans, to give you this land to possess . . .

"Know of a surety that your descendants will be sojourners in a land that is not theirs, and will be slaves there, and they will be oppressed for four hundred years; but I will bring judgment on the nation which they serve, and afterward they shall come out with great possessions. As for yourself, you shall go to your fathers in peace; you shall be buried in a good old age. And they shall come back here in the fourth generation; for the iniquity of the Amorites is not yet complete." . . . On that day the LORD made a covenant with Abram, saying, "To your descendants I give this land, from the river of Egypt to the great river, the river Euphrates."

(Gen. 15:1,4,5,7,13-16,18)

When Abram was 99 years old, God dealt with him again, restating the Covenant and changing his name to Abraham, meaning "father of a multitude." God then gave Abraham the sign of the Covenant, circumcision. But 24 years had passed since the promise had first been given, and Abraham still had no son by his wife Sarah.

When Abram was ninety-nine years old the LORD appeared to Abram, and said to him, "I am God

Almighty; walk before me, and be blameless. And I will make my covenant between me and you, and will multiply you exceedingly . . . Behold, my covenant is with you, and you shall be the father of a multitude of nations . . . I will make you exceedingly fruitful; and I will make nations of you, and kings shall come forth from you. And I will establish my covenant between me and you and your descendants after you throughout their generations for an ever-lasting covenant, to be God to you and to your descendants after you. And I will give to you, and to your descendants after you, the land of your sojournings, all the land of Canaan, for an ever-lasting possession; and I will be their God."

(Gen. 17:1,2,4,6-8)

And God said to Abraham, "As for Sarai your wife, you shall not call her name Sarai, but Sarah shall be her name. I will bless her, and moreover I will give you a son by her; I will bless her, and she shall be a mother of nations; kings of people shall come from her . . . Sarah your wife shall bear you a son, and you shall call his name Isaac. I will establish my covenant with him as an everlasting covenant for his descendants after him. As for Ishmael, I have heard you; behold, I will bless him and make him fruitful and multiply him exceedingly; he shall be the father of twelve princes, and I will make him a great nation. But I will establish my covenant with Isaac."

(Gen. 17:15,16,19-21)

> "I will indeed bless you, and I will multiply your
> descendants as the stars of heaven and as the sand
> which is on the seashore. And your descendants
> shall possess the gate of their enemies, and by your
> descendants shall all the nations of the earth bless
> themselves, because you have obeyed my voice."
> (Gen. 22:17,18)

All these blessings God promised to Abraham as the
LORD's part of the Covenant. But now, what was Abraham's
part in this Covenant? Since God was going to do so much
for him, what would Abraham be expected to fulfill?

Simply, there were no conditions required of Abraham.
He had no responsibility in the fulfillment of the Covenant.
God merely said, "I'm going to do these things for you and
for your descendants." Of course, the LORD did instruct
Abraham to be "blameless" before Him, and He commanded
circumcision as the outward sign of the Covenant. But the
Covenant did not depend upon Abraham's response to these
commands. The Covenant was valid regardless of Abraham's
obedience or disobedience. This Abrahamic Covenant, like
the Noahic Covenant before it, was purely unilateral,
unconditional.

But God knew Abraham's heart: "He believed the LORD;
and he reckoned it to him as righteousness" (Gen. 15:6).
This trust was later demonstrated in Gen. 22, when Abraham was willing to sacrifice his son and heir, Isaac, upon
the LORD's specific instruction.

Years later God spoke the same unilateral promise to Isaac.

> And the LORD appeared to him, and said,
> " . . . Sojourn in this land, and I will be with you,
> and will bless you; for to you and to your descen-
> dants I will give all these lands, and I will fulfil

the oath which I swore to Abraham your father. I will multiply your descendants as the stars of heaven, and will give to your descendants all these lands; and by your descendants all the nations of the earth shall bless themselves." (Gen. 26:2-4)

And the Lord appeared to him the same night and said, "I am the God of Abraham your father; fear not, for I am with you and will bless you and multiply your descendants for my servant Abraham's sake."   (Gen. 26:24)

And to Isaac's son, Jacob, God repeated his blessings—again and again.

And behold, the Lord stood above it and said, "I am the Lord, the God of Abraham your father and the God of Isaac; the land on which you lie I will give to you and to your descendants; and your descendants shall be like the dust of the earth, and you shall spread abroad to the west and to the east and to the north and to the south; and by you and your descendants shall all the families of the earth bless themselves. Behold, I am with you and will keep you wherever you go, and will bring you back to this land; for I will not leave you until I have done that of which I have spoken to you."
                                              (Gen. 28:13-15)

God appeared to Jacob again, when he came from Paddanaram, and blessed him. And God said to him, "Your name is Jacob; no longer shall your name be called Jacob, but Israel shall be your name." So his name was called Israel. And God said to him, "I am God Almighty: be fruitful and multiply; a nation and a company of nations shall come from you, and kings shall spring from you. The land which I gave to Abraham and Isaac I will give to you, and I will give the land to your descendants after you." (Gen. 35:9-12)

And God spoke to Israel in visions of the night, and said, "Jacob, Jacob." And he said, "Here am I." Then he said, "I am God, the God of your father; do not be afraid to go down to Egypt; for I will there make of you a great nation. I will go down with you to Egypt, and I will also bring you up again; and Joseph's hand shall close your eyes." (Gen. 46:2-4)

The fact that the Abrahamic Covenant, with its attendant blessings, is restated so many times, and to three successive generations, causes one to marvel at its importance among all the biblical covenants. Asaph's song sums up this sequence of eternal promises.

He is mindful of his covenant for ever, of the word that he commanded, for a thousand generations, the covenant which he made with Abraham, his sworn promise to Isaac, which he confirmed as a statute to Jacob, as an everlasting covenant to Israel, saying, "To you I will give the land of Canaan, as your portion for an inheritance." (1 Chron. 16:15-18)

Later we will see the quiet effects of this Covenant of Promise through the remainder of the Bible—indeed, through all of human history—and to this very day.

The Levitical Covenant

Now, let's move ahead about five centuries to investigate the next unilateral biblical covenant, known as the Levitical Covenant.

Under Moses' leadership, the Israelites had been wandering through the wilderness for nearly 40 years. At last, shortly before the death of Moses, Israel was encamped in the plains of Moab, preparing to cross the Jordan River. God had told Moses not to harm the Kingdom of Moab, so they had detoured eastward, through the desert, with the supply of manna still appearing faithfully every morning. Although Israel had promised not to attack or steal from them, the vast array of thousands of Hebrews, who had settled nearby temporarily with their tents and their large herds, frightened the pagan Moabites. The Moabite king complained of Israel that "they cover the face of the earth" (Numbers 22:5).

Further, the Moabites had already seen how Israel's army had destroyed their Amorite neighbors to the north. So the Moabite king, Balak, hired an enchanter, Balaam, to curse the Israelites. This tactic, of course, didn't work; God caused Balaam to bless Israel.

But Satan always has another strategy. The Israelites had eaten little but manna for 40 years, so they were doubly tempted, by normal food and by pretty girls. Numbers 25:1 says that "the people began to play the harlot with the daughters of Moab." Some of the Moabite girls invited the young men of Israel "to the sacrifices of their gods, and the people [of Israel] ate, and bowed down to their gods."

And the anger of the LORD was kindled against Israel; and the LORD said to Moses, "Take all the

> chiefs of the people, and hang them in the sun
> before the LORD, that the fierce anger of the LORD
> may turn away from Israel.'' And Moses said to the
> judges of Israel, ''Every one of you slay his men
> who have yoked themselves to Baal of Peor.''
> (Numbers 25:3-5)

This was harsh punishment, although such divine retributions had been shockingly frequent during those turbulent wilderness years.

Idolaters are usually quite bold. Apparently participating in the pagan Moabite religious rites was not enough sin to satisfy one Israelite. He brought the curse right into the camp.

> And behold, one of the people of Israel came and
> brought a Midianite woman to his family, in the
> sight of Moses and in the sight of the whole
> congregation of the people of Israel, while they
> were weeping at the door of the tent of meeting.

> When Phinehas the son of Eleazar, son of Aaron
> the priest, saw it, he rose and left the congrega-
> tion, and took a spear in his hand and went after
> the man of Israel into the inner room, and pierced
> both of them, the man of Israel and the woman,
> through her body. Thus the plague was stayed
> from the people of Israel. Nevertheless those that
> died by the plague were twenty-four thousand.
> (Numbers 25:6-9)

Again, vicious retribution. Yet out of that ugly event God proclaimed another of the fascinating biblical covenants.

> And the LORD said to Moses, "Phinehas the son
> of Eleazar, son of Aaron the priest, has turned back
> my wrath from the people of Israel, in that he was
> jealous with my jealousy among them, so that I
> did not consume the people of Israel in my jeal-
> ousy. Therefore say, 'Behold, I give to him my
> covenant of peace; and it shall be to him, and
> to his descendants after him, the covenant of a
> perpetual priesthood, because he was jealous for
> his God, and made atonement for the people of
> Israel.' "   (Numbers 25:10-13)

"The covenant of a perpetual priesthood!" That statement seems so casually made—almost hidden in the Book of Numbers—yet it was so rich with promise. While the Abrahamic Covenant is repeated again and again, as well as the Mosaic Covenant, the Covenant with Phinehas the priest is seldom mentioned in the Old Testament. There are only three other clear references to the Levitical Covenant.

First, we find that the LORD had earlier spoken about making this future Covenant to Aaron, the brother of Moses, the first high priest, a member of the tribe of Levi, and grand-father of the zealous Phinehas. God would often promise his covenant at a prior time, as in this case, followed by the covenant's actual ratification at a later date. The Noahic Covenant is such an example, where God told Noah of the impending Covenant before the Flood, but did not ratify it until after the Flood. So the Levitical Covenant was not actually established until Aaron's grandson, Phinehas, had boldly shed blood for the LORD. The LORD had already said to Aaron,

> "All the holy offerings which the people of Israel
> present to the LORD I give to you, and to your

sons and daughters with you, as a perpetual due;
it is a covenant of salt for ever before the Lord for
you and for your offspring with you.''

(Numbers 18:19)

A covenant of salt?

Again, God used terminology the Hebrews understood, although it may seem meaningless to us today. Ezra 4:14 refers to eating "the salt of the palace" in a letter to the king of Persia. In Semitic and neighboring cultures—even to this day—when a person has been invited to eat in a man's house, the host will defend his guest even at the cost of his own life. Witness Lot's being willing to give his own beloved virgin daughters to the evil homosexual mob that evening in Sodom, rather than allow the crowd to rape the two guests who had eaten in his home (Gen. 19). (See also Judges 19:22-24). Eating together in a Semitic home always created a covenant bond of loyalty—thus, a covenant of salt, as the food is salted.

When Jesus quoted from Psalms 41:9, "He who ate my bread has lifted his heel against me" (John 13:18), He was referring to a terrible act of betrayal—at least other Jews would have so perceived it—because Jesus and Judas Iscariot had been eating together at the Last Supper.

The making of a covenant normally involved eating a special meal together, as we have already seen. In all probability the elders of Israel ate with Moses and Aaron and his sons to celebrate this new priestly Covenant, although the Bible does not record such a banquet. Further, the Lord probably honored that covenant feast by coming down upon the sanctuary or the tent of meeting in the pillar of cloud and fire.

Leviticus 2:13 gives the solemn instructions that

> "You shall season all your cereal offerings with salt; you shall not let the salt of the covenant with your God be lacking from your cereal offering; with all your offerings you shall offer salt."

The salt was to be a continuing reminder of the Mosaic Covenant, reminding the Israelites and reminding the LORD.

God had also told the priests that the "holy offerings"—the food—was to be theirs "as a perpetual due." This meant that, as the Israelites would bring their tithe of animals or cereal to sacrifice to the LORD, the priests were to share in the eating of the food. This was to be one of the benefits of the Levitical Covenant for Aaron's priestly descendants—"the Covenant of salt." So the sharing in the eating of the sacrifices, as well as the eternal priesthood of Aaron's descendants, together constituted the blessings of the Levitical Covenant.

The shedding of sacrificial blood in the establishment of the Levitical Covenant apparently took place when Phinehas thrust his spear through both the Israelite and the Midianite woman. If there was a special animal sacrifice made at the LORD's instruction, such a sacrifice went unmentioned in the biblical narrative.

Later in the Old Testament we find only two other references that look back to this Covenant with Aaron, with his son Eleazar, his grandson Phinehas, and their descendants. First, Jeremiah gave a prophetic word involving the Covenant nearly a thousand years later, even as Jerusalem was about to be destroyed and its remaining citizens taken into captivity to Babylon.

"For thus says the LORD: David shall never lack a man to sit on the throne of the house of Israel, and the Levitical priests shall never lack a man in my presence to offer burnt offerings, to burn cereal offerings, and to make sacrifices for ever . . .

"Thus says the LORD: If you can break my covenant with the day and my covenant with the night, so that day and night will not come at their appointed time, then also my covenant with David my servant may be broken, so that he shall not have a son to reign on his throne, and my covenant with the Levitical priests my ministers. As the host of heaven cannot be numbered and the sands of the sea cannot be measured, so I will multiply the descendants of David my servant, and the Levitical priests who minister to me."

(Jer. 33:17-22)

This promise sounded so contradictory in the middle of the terrible siege of Jerusalem, but it would prove to be a great encouragement through the suffering of the years immediately ahead. So, even though the Covenant with the Levitical priests was established in a seemingly casual manner, yet, said the LORD, that Covenant will stand for ever.

A few centuries later, however, this promise was to lead to a serious concern for Jewish rabbis and scholars. Out of Aaron's descendants, one family later came to be the "high priestly" family. Yet this high priestly family died out less than a thousand years after Jeremiah's prophecy. The priestly lineage of Aaron has continued, however, as indicated by the common Jewish surname "Cohen" (Hebrew for "priest"). The rabbis were deeply troubled over the lack of an answer to the high priestly dilemma because they were looking for the wrong answer in the wrong place. We will discover the biblical answer later.

The final Old Testament reference to the Levitical Covenant is found in Malachi. This last book of the Old Testament was written prior to 400 B.C. The prophet Malachi said the LORD was concerned about some unethical behavior among the Jews, especially the priests. And the LORD also revealed through Malachi his expectations for the future. God there spoke particularly of the Old Testament covenants; He used that key word eight times in two chapters, alluding to at least three of the covenants in those eight references. The priests, the heirs to the Covenant with Aaron, were singled out for severe criticism.

> "And now, O priests, this command is for you . . . So shall you know that I have sent this command to you, that my covenant with Levi may hold, says the LORD of hosts. My covenant with him was a covenant of life and peace, and I gave them to him, that he might fear; and he feared me, he stood in awe of my name. True instruction was in his mouth, and no wrong was found on his lips. He walked with me in peace and uprightness, and he turned many from iniquity. For the lips of a priest should guard knowledge, and men should seek instruction from his mouth, for he is the messenger of the LORD of hosts.

> "But you have turned aside from the way; you have caused many to stumble by your instruction; you have corrupted the covenant of Levi, says the LORD of hosts, and so I make you despised and

> abased before all the people, inasmuch as you have
> not kept my ways but have shown partiality in
> your instruction.''   (Mal. 2:1,4-9)

This Covenant of blessing upon the sons of Aaron, the priests of Israel, is the third of the unilateral biblical covenants. Aaron, Eleazar and Phinehas could do nothing to earn God's blessing: they already had his blessing. Even in the midst of their false teaching and immorality, so denounced by Malachi, the priestly descendants of Aaron were still heirs to the Levitical promise; indeed, they could hardly reject the Covenant, even if they hadn't wanted it.

This points up a problem with unilateral blessings. Humans tend to take them for granted, and in the Bible we often see priests misleading God's People—from Aaron and the golden calf to the chief priests who orchestrated the crucifixion of Jesus. Even then, God remains faithful to his Levitical Promise!

The Davidic Covenant

And God ordained yet another unilateral covenant! 500 years following the establishment of the Levitical Covenant, David was king over all Israel. He had built himself a pleasant palace; and 2 Samuel 7:1 says that '' . . . the LORD had given him rest from all his enemies round about.'' So,

> . . . the king said to Nathan the prophet, "See now,
> I dwell in a house of cedar, but the ark of God
> dwells in a tent." And Nathan said to the king,
> "Go, do all that is in your heart; for the LORD is
> with you."

But that same night the word of the LORD came to Nathan, ''Go and tell my servant David, 'Thus says the LORD: Would you build me a house to dwell in? I have not dwelt in a house since the day I brought up the people of Israel from Egypt to this day, but I have been moving about in a tent for my dwelling. In all places where I have moved with all the people of Israel, did I speak a word with any of the judges of Israel, whom I commanded to shepherd my people Israel, saying, ''Why have you not built me a house of cedar?'' '

''Now therefore thus you shall say to my servant David, 'Thus says the LORD of hosts, I took you from the pasture, from following the sheep, that you should be prince over my people Israel; and I have been with you wherever you went, and have cut off all your enemies from before you; and I will make for you a great name, like the name of the great ones of the earth. And I will appoint a place for my people Israel, and will plant them, that they may dwell in their own place, and be disturbed no more; and violent men shall afflict them no more, as formerly, from the time that I appointed judges over my people Israel; and I will give you rest from all your enemies.

'' 'Moreover the LORD declares to you that the LORD will make you a house. When your days are fulfilled and you lie down with your fathers, I will raise up your offspring after you, who shall come forth from your body, and I will establish his kingdom. He shall build a house for my name, and I will establish the throne of his kingdom for ever.

I will be his father, and he shall be my son. When he commits iniquity, I will chasten him with the rod of men, with the stripes of the sons of men; but I will not take my steadfast love from him, as I took it from Saul, whom I put away from before you.

" 'And your house and your kingdom shall be made sure for ever before me; your throne shall be established for ever.' " In accordance with all these words, and in accordance with all this vision, Nathan spoke to David. (2 Sam. 7:2-17)

The key verses are 5, 11 and 16. "Would you build *me* a house to dwell in? . . . The LORD declares to you that the LORD will make *you* a house . . . And your house and your kingdom shall be made sure for ever before me; your throne shall be established for ever."

What did He mean when God spoke of making a house for David?

God was describing what we call a dynasty, as the House of Windsor, the royal house of Britain, or the House of Hapsburg, the former royal house of Austria. And God did just that: King Saul had no descendants on the throne of Israel, but David's descendants sat on the throne for many generations.

The word "covenant" does not appear in God's promise to David in 2 Samuel 7, but later scriptures refer back to the event in covenant terminology. David composed an "oracle" late in his life.

"Yea, does not my house stand so with God? For he has made with me an everlasting covenant, ordered in all things and secure."   (2 Samuel 23:5)

Psalms 89 clearly states the LORD's Covenant promise to David.

> "My steadfast love I will keep for him for ever, and my covenant will stand firm for him. I will establish his line for ever and his throne as the days of the heavens. If his children forsake my law and do not walk according to my ordinances, if they violate my statutes and do not keep my commandments, then I will punish their transgression with the rod and their iniquity with scourges; but I will not remove from him my steadfast love, or be false to my faithfulness. I will not violate my covenant, or alter the word that went forth from my lips.

> "Once for all I have sworn by my holiness; I will not lie to David. His line shall endure for ever, his throne as long as the sun before me. Like the moon it shall be established for ever; it shall stand firm while the skies endure." (Psalms 89:28-37)

The Davidic Covenant is mentioned again and again in the Old Testament, sometimes explicitly, other times by implication. We have already noted Jeremiah's prophecy, including both Covenants, Levitical and Davidic.

> "For thus says the LORD: David shall never lack a man to sit on the throne of the house of Israel, and the Levitical priests shall never lack a man in my presence to offer burnt offerings, to burn cereal offerings, and to make sacrifices for ever."

> The word of the LORD came to Jeremiah: "Thus says the LORD: If you can break my covenant with the day and my covenant with the night, so that

day and night will not come at their appointed time, then also my covenant with David my servant may be broken, so that he shall not have a son to reign on his throne, and my covenant with the Levitical priests my ministers. As the host of heaven cannot be numbered and the sands of the sea cannot be measured, so I will multiply the descendants of David my servant, and the Levitical priests who minister to me."

(Jer. 33:17-22)

The Davidic Covenant is also described as a covenant of salt.

"The LORD God of Israel gave the kingship of Israel for ever to David and his sons by a covenant of salt." (2 Chron. 13:5)

Once again we see a unilateral Covenant. God demanded nothing of David regarding a conditional response in order to fulfill this Covenant. The LORD merely said, "I will establish your descendants on the throne of Israel for ever."

The story of David indicates how God chooses a man to bless with a unilateral covenant. He is quite careful in whom He selects. The LORD had commanded the prophet Samuel to go to the home of Jesse, in Bethlehem, and there anoint one of Jesse's sons to be king over Israel in place of the disappointing King Saul. When Samuel saw Jesse's eldest son, he observed quickly how handsome Eliab appeared, and how tall and strong he was. Samuel thought, "Surely this young man is the one God has anointed to be the new king!"

But the LORD said to Samuel, "Do not look on his appearance or on the height of his stature, because I have rejected him; for the LORD sees not as man

sees; man looks on the outward appearance,
but the LORD looks on the heart."

(1 Samuel 16:7)

And so Samuel met all seven of Jesse's sons, and the LORD
rejected every one in turn.

And Samuel said to Jesse, "Are all your sons here?"
And he said, "There remains yet the youngest, but
behold, he is keeping the sheep." And Samuel said
to Jesse, "Send and fetch him; for we will not sit
down till he comes here." And he sent, and
brought him in.   (1 Sam. 16:11,12)

As soon as Samuel saw the teenage David, the LORD said,
"Arise, anoint him; for this is he." God knew David's heart,
just as He knew Abraham's heart, and Noah's and Phinehas'
as well.

There are several delightfully-descriptive names which
indicate the special relationships between these men and
the God who chose them. "But Noah found favor in the
eyes of the LORD" (Gen. 6:8). "Didst thou not, O our God,
drive out the inhabitants of this land before thy people Israel,
and give it for ever to the descendants of Abraham thy
friend?" (2 Chron. 20:7). "But you, Israel, my servant,
. . . the offspring of Abraham, my friend . . . " (Isaiah 41:8).
"Abraham believed God, . . . and he was called the friend
of God" (James 2:23). "The LORD has sought out a man
after his own heart [David]; and the LORD has appointed
him to be prince over his people" (1 Sam. 13:14). "I have
found in David the son of Jesse a man after my heart, who
will do all my will" (Acts 13:22).

David had such a great respect for God's anointed ruler
that he refused to retaliate against Saul, even when the

jealous king was seeking to kill him. God protected the young man through many narrow escapes, honoring his commitment to make David king over Israel. And, of course, under David's subsequent rule, Israel began to flower into the nation God had promised Abraham, Isaac and Jacob, as well as Moses and the people of Israel in the wilderness.

Nevertheless, in the years to follow, David was faithless in that he committed a terrible crime by having Uriah killed in order to take Uriah's wife, Bathsheba, for himself. Later, David was also faithless in that he did not restrain his own sons during all the tragic palace intrigues, ultimately costing the lives of three of those young men. David became a rather ineffectual ruler during his latter years, ignoring many of the kingly responsibilities which his sons Absalom and Adonijah, each in his turn, quietly seized for themselves. Yet God's promise remained valid; neither of David's ambitious sons succeeded in his rebellion.

We might ask then, What effect upon God's covenants is provoked by the behavior or misbehavior of the heirs to the covenants? Let's investigate.

When Does a Biblical Covenant End?

We need to understand how long God's Old Testament covenants remain in force. Do they terminate at some point? Have they all been superseded by the New Covenant in Jesus Christ? Has the unfaithfulness of the majority of the Jewish people brought about the withdrawal of God's blessings? Has the Christian Church become the "New Israel" because of God's rejection of the "Old Israel"?

Let's investigate by examining what is today the most controversial blessing of all, God's promise to Abram in Genesis 15:18.

> On that day the LORD made a covenant with Abram, saying, "To your descendants I give this land, from the river of Egypt to the great river, the river Euphrates."

Many people today, including some misguided Christians, are demanding that Israel "give back" the West Bank to Jordan.

First, to set the record straight, the West Bank never belonged to Jordan: they arbitrarily seized it when the British departed shortly after World War II.

But that is not the real question. Who owns the Land? whether we call it Palestine, or Israel, or Occupied Arab Territory, or the Holy Land, or the Land of Promise? Who owns it? The psalmist answers.

> The earth is the LORD's and the fulness thereof, the world and those who dwell therein.
>
> (Psalms 24:1)

> The Most High gave to the nations their inheritance, when He separated the sons of men, He fixed the bounds of the peoples.
>
> (Deut. 32:8)

The Land belongs to God, and He gives it to whom He chooses! It's quite simple. Therefore, said God to Abram, "To your descendants I give this land."

That gift can create a problem of interpretation. Perhaps 99% of the people living in the Holy Land *are* direct descendants of Abraham, many of them through Ishmael, Abraham's son by Sarah's maid, Hagar, as well as by his other concubine, Keturah. Yet Abraham's children are still fighting between the various families: "We own it!" "No! It's ours!"

Christians who claim that Ishmael's descendants are also children of Abraham, and thus have a right to the Land, should read the Bible more carefully.

> God said, "As for Ishmael, . . . I will bless him and make him fruitful . . . But I will establish my covenant with Isaac."   (Gen. 17:20,21)

> Abraham gave all that he had to Isaac. But to the sons of his concubines Abraham gave gifts, and while he was still living he sent them away from his son Isaac, eastward to the east country.
>   (Gen. 25:5,6)

> Not all are children of Abraham because they are his descendants; but "Through Isaac shall your descendants be named."   (Romans 9:7)

Later, the Lord repeated the promise to Isaac, but not to Ishmael, or to his other half-brothers.

> "I will multiply your descendants as the stars of heaven, and will give to your descendants all these lands."   (Gen. 26:4)

All these scriptures immediately eliminate the Arabs who are descended from Abraham's concubines from any God-given inheritance in the Land of Israel. Their inheritance is "eastward to the east country." There they may have all the oil they could possibly desire. The inheritance of the Land is through Isaac.

But, it could be protested, Isaac had two sons, Esau and Jacob (Gen. 25:5,6). Esau was the father of the Edomites, most of whose descendants were forcibly amalgamated with the Jews prior to the time of Herod the Great (who was an Edomite married to a Jewess), which almost makes this question moot. We might speculate that God wished to bless Jacob's twin brother by incorporating Esau's descendants into the Chosen People. The remnant of Edomites who may have resisted the forced conversion to Judaism (about 100 B.C.) were probably later blended into the general Arab population. Does the Land then belong also to the line of Esau? We look again to the scripture, where God spoke to Isaac's son, Jacob, renamed by God as "Israel."

> "The land which I gave to Abraham and Isaac I
> will give to you, and I will give the land to your
> descendants after you."   (Gen. 35:12)

And that eliminates everybody except the descendants of Israel. Therefore, as Esau's descendants were gradually woven into Israel, they too received the blessing. That special Land—like the rest of the earth—belongs to God, and He has given it to the children of Israel!

But, has God rescinded this Abrahamic Covenant because of the unfaithfulness of most of the Patriarchs' descendants?

Many Christians have taught so. Augustine, about A.D. 400, made this a doctrine, and the Church has more or less followed his understanding. The ill will between Christians and Jews ran deep in those early centuries of the Church. For more than 250 years the Christian Church was to the Roman Empire *religio illicita*, and Jews often denounced their Christian relatives and neighbors to the Roman authorities, leading to much suffering and death for Christians. Perceiving God's love for the Jews would have been extremely difficult for Christian leaders during these early centuries, for many Jews considered Christianity to be nothing more than a heresy of Judaism. The idea that God's covenant blessings have been withdrawn from the Jews has contributed to the anti-Semitism of past centuries, and to the recent pogroms in eastern Europe and the holocaust in Nazi Germany.

Today cooler heads prevail. Besides, we will find that the Jews' period of punishment is now ending. The Holy Spirit is speaking a message of love for the Jews into Christian hearts today, although non-Christians seem to be getting more hostile. Christians are expressing a concern for the nation of Israel such as never before. This is indeed the Holy Spirit's work in our modern world. Augustine was wrong. Were he writing today, more than 1500 years later, Augustine would not be proposing such an unscriptural doctrine.

We may search the Bible from beginning to end, and we will not find one statement suggesting that God has retracted the gift of the Land to the descendants of Israel! True, there was a God-ordained time of "sabbaths" for the Land, but that period has been concluded. Although Jesus said—

> "I tell you, many will come from east and west
> and sit at table with Abraham, Isaac, and Jacob in
> the kingdom of heaven, while the sons of the king-
> dom will be thrown into the outer darkness; there
> men will weep and gnash their teeth,"
> (Matt. 8:11,12)

—this still does not invalidate God's permanent gift of the Land to Israel.

How tragic that many liberal Christians (and some conservatives) hold to the Church's traditional view concerning Israel, a view born out of religious hostility and persecution, in spite of the clear biblical testimony to the contrary! God is a Zionist! His Covenant with Abraham is irrevocable!

> "And I will give to you, and to your descendants
> after you, the land of your sojournings, all the land
> of Canaan, for an everlasting possession; and I will
> be their God." (Gen. 17:8)

Still further, beyond the Abrahamic Covenant, God also promised the same national boundaries in the *other* major Old Testament Covenant, the Mosaic Covenant! And He renewed that promise to Joshua.

> "Every place that the sole of your foot will tread
> upon I have given to you, as I promised to Moses.
> From the wilderness and this Lebanon as far as the
> great river, the river Euphrates, all the land of the
> Hittites to the Great Sea toward the going down
> of the sun shall be your territory." (Joshua 1:3,4)

Those Christians who demand that Israel "give back" any land to the Arabs are resisting the will of the God who has chosen to bless Israel anew in our generation. The Abrahamic Covenant stands valid to this day, and that Promise has blossomed more beautifully in the centuries since the writing of the Old Testament. But that remains for a later chapter.

When does a biblical covenant end? The remainder of this book is dedicated to answering that question.

The Land of the Covenants

Now the question we may ask is, What are the boundaries of the Land of Promise?

To Abraham God first described its parameters: " . . . from the river of Egypt to the great river, the river Euphrates."

Nobody is quite certain what river was intended by "the river of Egypt." It was not the Red Sea, because neither the Red Sea nor its northern arms, the Gulf of Aqaba and the Gulf of Suez, are rivers. These saltwater bodies could not possibly be what was intended by "the river of Egypt." The *southern* tip of the Promised Land is later specifically noted to be the "Red Sea" (Exodus 23:31); this point would be the Red Sea's northeastern arm, the Gulf of Aqaba, which incidentally does form today's southern boundary of Israel, at Elath.

Some scholars think "the river of Egypt" is "the Brook of Egypt," today known as the Wadi El Arish, situated southwest of the Gaza Strip. But the Hebrew word for "river" is *nihar*, while the word for "brook" is *nahal*. Further, the Brook of Egypt contains water only during the rainy season, when the Sinai highlands fill it with occasional torrents.

"The river of Egypt" presents another possibility—the Nile River. The ancient town of Pelusium, near the northern terminus of the modern Suez Canal, was quite close to the eastern edge of the Nile delta. Could the Nile River delta at Pelusium be one of the ancient boundaries of the Land of the Promise, the southwestern corner?

Still, there is a further problem. This southwestern geographical reference point is not consistent in the scriptures. In Numbers 34:1-12 God gave Moses more detailed boundaries for the Land of Promise. There God stated plainly, "the Brook of Egypt"—the Wadi El Arish. And this does seem to be a more appropriate boundary line. Yet, there remains the discrepancy with the earlier Abrahamic promise in Genesis. And so, some scholars have proposed "a copyist's error" many centuries ago in Genesis 15:18, where the correction of only one Hebrew letter could make "river" read "brook." This explanation makes sense. However, we are not absolutely certain of the precise southwestern corner.

The northeastern corner, God told Abraham, is "the great river, the river Euphrates." Today that point of the boundary would probably be in eastern Syria, near where the Euphrates River flows into Iraq. That is a long way beyond the northeastern border of modern Israel.

We must look elsewhere in the Old Testament to locate other boundaries for the Land of Promise. Having already noted Numbers 34:1-12, let's follow that boundary line.

God was very careful to avoid giving the territories of Edom, Moab and Ammon to the Israelites. The LORD had long since given these lands to those founding "relatives" of Israel. Moab and Ammon were the sons of Lot, and Edom was established by Jacob's brother, Esau. Edom was south of the Land of Promise, Moab to the southeast, and Ammon to the east. Israel could not have these lands.

The western boundary of the Land of Promise would be "the Great Sea," the Mediterranean Sea. The northern boundary was to be the "entrance of Hamath." No one is certain as to precisely where the entrance of Hamath was to be found. The Kingdom of Hamath lay to the north of Israel; its capital, present-day Hamah, is in Syria, well north of Damascus. The entrance of Hamath probably meant the southern boundary of that kingdom. If so, it would lie somewhere in the Bekaa Valley of eastern Lebanon, an area very much in the news in recent years. Other northern boundary points mentioned in Numbers 34 are unidentifiable today.

So the northern boundary ran from the Euphrates River west to the Bekaa Valley, then to the southwest, avoiding the Phoenician cities of Tyre and Sidon, to the Mediterranean Sea.

The northeastern boundary appears to have included the Golan Heights and the upper Jordan River Valley. Israel under Moses did also conquer and occupy the two Amorite kingdoms in that area on the eastern side of the Jordan before crossing the river at Jericho.

We should note that King Solomon's dominion, if we include vassal kingdoms and dual monarchies, extended to these prophesied boundaries, and also included the nations of Ammon, Moab and Edom. Today, God's promised boundaries would add to the territory controlled by modern Israel perhaps the southern third of Syria (including Damascus, which will some day be permanently destroyed, as described in Isaiah 17:1,2), a small portion of southeastern Lebanon, and a narrow slice of the northern Sinai currently occupied by Egypt.

This is God's Land, the Land of his Promise. The living God still retains the privilege of deciding whose is the Land. He long ago gave it to Israel by a Covenant which cannot be broken. The major portion of the Land not yet under Israeli control lies in sabre-rattling Syria. Will we see God restore the biblical boundaries to Israel in our day?

This problem began 3400 years ago with Israel's disobedience after the death of Joshua. God's People simply got tired of war. Israel didn't complete the conquest as they had been solemnly instructed. After Joshua's death only the tribes of Judah and Simeon continued to conquer their allotted inheritances in the southern part of the Land of Promise.

The tribe of Dan couldn't dislodge the Philistines from their assigned area, so they later migrated north, near the entrance of Hamath, and in a lightning attack destroyed and occupied a community that had been under the suzerainty of Sidon of the Phoenicians. Other tribes had very little success in defeating their Canaanite neighbors in the plains, since the Canaanites knew the technology of iron working, and their iron chariots normally overwhelmed the Israelite warriors.

So God's solemn warning not to settle down beside the pagans went unheeded—to Israel's everlasting sorrow. As the result of his intimate dealings with pagan states, creating unholy marriage alliances, even the wise King Solomon drifted into polytheism in his old age. Therefore, as punishment for Solomon's terrible sin, God split the Kingdom into two parts—Judah and Benjamin in the south, and the rest of the tribes, known as "Israel," to the north. Finally He allowed the idolatrous Northern Kingdom, Israel, to be destroyed, and later drove Judah into exile because of their persistent disobedience. "For the Lord disciplines him whom He loves" (Hebrews 12:6).

Did all of this rebellion and disobedience terminate the blessings of the unilateral covenants? For centuries countless Christian theologians have taught so. But let's review the Davidic Covenant as recorded in Psalms 89:30-34.

> "If his children forsake my law and do not walk according to my ordinances, if they violate my statutes and do not keep my commandments, then I will punish their transgression with the rod and their iniquity with scourges; but I will not remove from him my steadfast love, or be false to my faithfulness. I will not violate my covenant, or alter the word that went forth from my lips."

Notice again the final sentence: "I will not violate my covenant, or alter the word that went forth from my lips"— whether they are faithful or not.

The psalmist, writing after the terrible destruction and suffering of the Exile, brought this psalm up-to-date as he surveyed the ruins of once-beautiful Jerusalem. The psalmist is so disconsolate that he thinks God has renounced the heirs to the Davidic Covenant.

> But now thou hast cast off and rejected, thou art full of wrath against thy anointed. Thou hast renounced the covenant with thy servant; thou hast defiled his crown in the dust. Thou hast breached all his walls; thou hast laid his strongholds in ruins . . . How long, O Lord? Wilt thou hide thyself for ever? How long will thy wrath burn like fire? . . . Lord, where is thy steadfast love of old, which by thy faithfulness thou didst swear to David? (Psalms 89:38-40,46,49)

Indeed, God did seem briefly to have rejected the Davidic Covenant. Yet the Temple was rebuilt before the end of the very century in which it had been destroyed (see Haggai), and Jerusalem's walls were rebuilt a generation-or-two later under Nehemiah. God's pledges always bring the promised restoration. His punishment is only for a time for those whom He loves, although it might seem an eternity to finite man. The Old City of Jerusalem has been under foreign domination (except for a brief and troublous hundred years in the second and first centuries B.C.) ever since Nebuchadnezzar destroyed the city—until A.D. 1967 in this present generation—2555 years. The land was "enjoying its sabbaths" for a very long time.

God even gave a biblical formula for ascertaining the length of Jerusalem's "sabbath."

> "According to the number of the days in which
> you spied out the land, forty days, for every day
> a year, you shall bear your iniquity, forty years,
> and you shall know my displeasure."
>
> (Numbers 14:34)

Remember the words, "for every day a year." The formula
is found by coupling together this scripture from Numbers
14 with Leviticus 26 as it spells out the curses for disobedience. The curses are terrible. Four times in that chapter
God said they would be punished "sevenfold."

> "And if in spite of this you will not hearken to me,
> then I will chastise you again *sevenfold* for your
> sins . . . And I will scatter you among the nations,
> and I will unsheathe the sword after you; and your
> land shall be a desolation, and your cities shall be
> a waste. Then the land shall pay for its sabbaths
> as long as it lies desolate, while you are in your
> enemies' land; then the land shall rest, and enjoy
> its sabbaths."   (Lev. 26:18,33,34)

Recall the formula from Numbers—"for every day a year"
of punishment. There are 365 days in a year. Then, the
punishment period is to be multiplied sevenfold, or 365
times seven, which equals 2,555 years of punishment.
Nebuchadnezzar destroyed the city in 587 B.C. and Jerusalem (the Old City) was recovered in A.D. 1967, which equals
2,554 years. Add one for the "zero year" between B.C. and
A.D., and there we find the assigned "sabbath" period for
Jerusalem.

The same numerical results can be obtained by using also
the predictions of Jeremiah 16:18 and Revelation 11:1,2.
According to Revelation 11 (see also Luke 21:24), the nations

(Gentiles) "will trample over the holy city for 42 months." Jeremiah 16:18 says, "I will *doubly* recompense their iniquity and their sin." 42 months doubled is 84 months (seven years). Coupling this figure with Numbers 14 ("for every day a year"), 365 days times seven is once again 2,555 years of the holy city's being trampled by the nations, with its "sabbaths" ending precisely in 1967, the year the Israelis retook the Old City of Jerusalem.

The biblical numerics are unimportant, although some Bible students find great pleasure in such formulas. The point, however, is that God chastens those whom He loves, and the chastening can be violent at times, and even prolonged. Still He remains ever faithful to his covenants; the punishment will come to an end.

> "Yet for all that, when they are in the land of their enemies, I will not spurn them, neither will I abhor them so as to destroy them utterly and break my covenant with them; for I am the LORD their God; but I will for their sake remember the covenant with their forefathers, whom I brought forth out of the land of Egypt in the sight of the nations that I might be their God: I am the LORD."
>
> (Lev. 26:44,45)

Today, as that biblical period of punishment has now ended, many Jews are once again in their independent homeland, although not in possession of all of it yet. Many more Jews will be coming soon, especially from the Soviet Union, "the land of the north."

> "In those days the house of Judah shall join the house of Israel, and together they shall come from

> the land of the north to the land that I gave your
> fathers for a heritage." (Jer. 3:18)

The living God is still very much at work. He has "signed"
his Name to the Abrahamic Covenant.

Contradictory Covenants

We see in the Old Testament this strange paradox of God's
promise to *bless* Israel according to the unilateral covenants
and his promise to *punish* Israel for breaking the bilateral
Mosaic Covenant. This puzzling contradiction has historically caused much indecision, anguish and re-thinking by
the Chosen People. How do you resolve the questions, Will
we be blessed by God because of his faithfulness to the
unconditional Abrahamic Covenant? or, Will we be cursed
by God because of our disobedience to the conditional
Mosaic Covenant? Much tragedy occurred in Israel because
they could not answer those questions correctly.

The clash between these two covenant traditions nearly
destroyed Israel. Had it not been for the faithfulness of the
God of the covenants, the Chosen People would have been
no more than a tiny parenthesis in human history. The Old
Testament drama builds toward a catastrophic collapse of
the divine purpose.

Again, the primary example of this problem focuses on
the holy city. Let's look at more of Jerusalem's history.

Having recently destroyed the Northern Kingdom, Israel,
in 721 B.C., the Assyrians under King Sennacherib later
moved on to attack the Southern Kingdom, Judah. Hezekiah was the good, reforming king of Judah, but the powerful Assyrian army quickly conquered almost all of the nation

except the capital. Most of the Judahites had already abandoned Jerusalem because of their fear that it would fall to the Assyrians, who incidentally were very cruel soldiers.

One of the chief officers of King Sennacherib stood outside the wall of Jerusalem and mockingly suggested a wager with King Hezekiah: "I will give you two thousand horses, if you are able on your part to set riders upon them" (2 Kings 18:23). The Assyrian commander knew that there were very few loyal soldiers remaining inside the walls of Jerusalem. But Hezekiah refused to surrender. Instead, he performed an act quite unlike most human rulers. The king went into the Temple and prayed,

> "Incline thy ear, O LORD, and hear; open thy eyes, O LORD, and see; and hear the words of Sennacherib, which he has sent to mock the living God . . . So now, O LORD our God, save us, I beseech thee, from his hand, that all the kingdoms of the earth may know that thou, O LORD, art God alone." (2 Kings 19:16,19)

Then the word of the LORD came to Isaiah the prophet. Here are some of the ominous predictions God gave Isaiah for the Assyrian Sennacherib.

> Therefore the Lord, the LORD of hosts, will send wasting sickness among his stout warriors, and under his glory a burning will be kindled, like the burning of fire. (Isa. 10:16)

> "Behold, I will put a spirit in him so that he shall hear a rumor and return to his own land;

and I will cause him to fall by the sword in his own land . . .

"Because you have raged against me and your arrogance has come into my ears, I will put my hook in your nose and my bit in your mouth, and I will turn you back on the way by which you came . . .

"By the way that he came, by the same he shall return, and he shall not come into this city, says the LORD. For I will defend this city to save it, for my own sake and for the sake of my servant David."   (2 Kings 19:7,28,33,34)

There we see God's acknowledgment of the unconditional Davidic Covenant. Hezekiah was almost totally defenseless; a handful of Assyrians could have captured Jerusalem. But the LORD remained faithful.

And that night the angel of the LORD went forth, and slew a hundred and eight-five thousand in the camp of the Assyrians; and when men arose early in the morning, behold, these were all dead bodies. Then Sennacherib king of Assyria departed, and went home, and dwelt at Nineveh. And as he was worshiping in the house of Nisroch his god, Adrammelech and Sharezer, his sons, slew him with the sword, and escaped into the land of Ararat. And Esarhaddon his son reigned in his stead.   (2 Kings 19:35-37)

We don't know how the LORD accomplished that "terrible" miracle, but every word of Isaiah's prophecies came true.

The bulk of Sennacherib's army, encamped before Jerusalem, died during one night. The King James Version of 2 Kings 19:7 translates the Hebrew word *ruach* as "blast": "Behold, I will send a blast upon him . . . " The Hebrew word means "spirit," but it can also mean "air" or "wind," as in a blast furnace for steelmaking. Was it a sudden epidemic, or food poisoning, or a destruction from the skies? We simply do not know; Judah's historians were too brief. The "wasting sickness" of Isaiah 10:16 is our only hint. It certainly reminds us of the tenth plague in Egypt, when the angel of the Lord killed all the firstborn sons of Egypt during the night of the Passover (Exodus 12:29).

By whatever means God destroyed 185,000 Assyrian soldiers, He was spectacularly faithful to his unconditional Covenants with Abraham and David! In fact, in the writings of Isaiah the prophet, where the Abrahamic and Davidic Covenants are so prominent, the bilateral, conditional Mosaic Covenant is never mentioned.

If the nation of Judah had ever doubted that God was true to his promises, those doubts were powerfully dispelled by this dramatic event, right outside the walls of Jerusalem. A last-minute deliverance is so typical of the LORD! Isaiah the prophet and King Hezekiah must have become national heroes! The unilateral covenants had been vindicated!

But what about the punishments promised for Israel's violations of the Mosaic Covenant? Did the Abrahamic and Davidic Covenants overrule the bilateral Covenant?

To answer that question, let's move ahead, a little more than a century later. The date was 588 B.C. The city was the same, but a different king, Zedekiah, sat on the throne of Judah. A different enemy, Nebuchadnezzar, king of the Babylonians, with his army, had surrounded the walls of Jerusalem. Jeremiah was the prophet of God.

The LORD was speaking this time through Jeremiah, proclaiming destruction for Jerusalem and death or exile for God's rebellious People. Judah's priests and nobles must have repeatedly reminded Jeremiah of God's great deliverance more than a hundred years before. "The LORD will always be faithful to his Covenants with Abraham and David!" they surely proclaimed to Jeremiah. Certainly they referred also to King Jehoshaphat's incredible deliverance from the armies of three allied nations nearly three hundred years earlier (2 Chron. 20).

If we may put words in Jeremiah's mouth, the prophet might have said, "This time is different! The LORD is not dealing with you according to the unilateral Covenants, Abrahamic and Davidic. Rather, He is dealing with you today according to the bilateral Covenant, the Ten Commandments, the conditional Covenant your fathers agreed to at Mt. Sinai."

The other prophets of Jerusalem were enraged! Jeremiah was rebuffed, beaten and locked up on several occasions. This narrative points up a situation that has developed repeatedly throughout the centuries among God's people. For every true prophet of God, there are at least 50 false prophets who tell people what they want to hear (see 1 Kings 18:17-22). And the false prophets always have "evidence" to back up their claims, as we see they did in Jerusalem in 588 B.C. The false prophets did indeed have a strong case. After all, had not God said the last time Jerusalem was attacked,

" . . . For I will defend this city to save it, for my
own sake and for the sake of my servant David"?
(2 Kings 19:34)

So Jeremiah was considered by the nation's leaders to be not only a false prophet, but an unpatriotic traitor. Once he was jailed as he was leaving the city, accused of deserting to the king of Babylon (Jer. 37:13-15).

Judah's King Zedekiah probably intended to be a good ruler, but he was a weak leader. He would schedule a private audience with the jailed Jeremiah, because he knew Jeremiah was a genuine prophet of God. But the influential men of the city—the nobles, the priests, the false prophets— were too powerful for King Zedekiah to withstand.

God spoke to his People again and again, primarily through this one prophet, Jeremiah, who came from a prominent family of priests. Even his own priestly relatives treated Jeremiah with contempt, and he pleaded with God to stop giving him these terrible prophecies of doom.

> O LORD, thou hast deceived me, and I was deceived; thou art stronger than I, and thou hast prevailed. I have become a laughingstock all the day; every one mocks me. For whenever I speak, I cry out, I shout, "Violence and destruction!" For the word of the LORD has become for me a reproach and derision all day long. If I say, "I will not mention him, or speak any more in his name," there is in my heart as it were a burning fire shut up in my bones, and I am weary with holding it in, and I cannot. (Jer. 20:7-9)

Another time King Zedekiah begged Jeremiah to give him an encouraging word based upon the unilateral covenants.

> "Inquire of the LORD for us . . . ; perhaps the LORD will deal with us according to all his wonderful deeds, and will make [Nebuchadnezzar] withdraw from us." (Jer. 21:2)

But God's answer was negative, indeed, frightening. Again Jeremiah pleaded fruitlessly with King Zedekiah: "Only if Judah will repent of its sins and surrender to Nebuchadnezzar will the LORD protect you." No wonder Jeremiah was treated as a false prophet and an unpatriotic deserter! Ever since the LORD's remarkable deliverance a century earlier, the unilateral covenant tradition had been so strong that God's People couldn't deal with the "contradictory" Mosaic Covenant.

So the LORD, in great anger over his own People's persistent faithlessness, finally turned them over to the furious wrath of the Babylonian army. As Jeremiah had said, God did indeed judge this time according to the conditional Mosaic Covenant. And the surviving remnant of Judah *walked*—in chains—the hundreds of miles into Babylonian slavery. Even the precious, holy Ark of the Covenant was destroyed—for ever. Jeremiah had predicted its demise also.

> "They shall no more say, 'The ark of the covenant of the LORD.' It shall not come to mind, or be remembered, or missed; it shall not be made again."
> (Jer. 3:16)

Even the Ark itself had become an idolatrous symbol in Judah.

For all of Jeremiah's anguish and frustration, he still was a prophet of *hope*. Again and again—in the midst of his doleful predictions—Jeremiah would tell about God's great plans for Israel's eventual future. His words seem so contradictory. But this is the way God deals with his disobedient Covenant People: He always promises to restore them after his anger subsides.

"They shall be carried to Babylon and remain there until the day when I give attention to them, says the LORD. Then I will bring them back and restore them to this place." (Jer. 27:22)

"And it shall come to pass that as I have watched over them to pluck up and break down, to overthrow, destroy, and bring evil, so I will watch over them to build and to plant, says the LORD." (Jer. 31:28)

In the midst of chaos, destruction, killing and burning—all over Judah—God used Jeremiah to reaffirm a promise He had made long before.

Thus says the LORD, who gives the sun for light by day and the fixed order of the moon and the stars for light by night, who stirs up the sea so that its waves roar—the LORD of hosts is his name: "If this fixed order departs from before me, says the LORD, then shall the descendants of Israel cease from being a nation before me for ever." Thus says the LORD: "If the heavens above can be measured, and the foundations of the earth below can be explored, then I will cast off all the descendants of Israel for all that they have done, says the LORD." (Jer. 31:35-37)

Even without a homeland, the Jews have been kept by God wherever they have wandered since that terrible day when a remnant was taken into captivity by Nebuchadnezzar more than 2500 years ago, and also since that later day when, in July of A.D. 70, the angry Romans scattered the Jews across the earth. God's Covenant with Abraham violates all the rules of human history. No other nation has ever survived without a homeland! Thus, our Creator-God is Lord of history. King Frederick the Great of Prussia was said to have asked his court preacher to give him just one proof that God exists. The preacher responded, "The Jew, your Majesty!" And the king agreed.

A number of scholars, both Jewish and Gentile, have written books and articles on "the indomitable Jewish spirit" that has kept this People intact through the centuries. Although their explanations are valid to a point, the real reason is God's Promise. The LORD is faithful to his covenants!

The question, Who owns the Land? is very much tied to this "Dual Covenant" paradox. Since the Abrahamic Covenant clearly gives the Promised Land to Israel for ever, as Gen. 15:18 says,

> "To your descendants I give this land, from the river of Egypt to the great river, the river Euphrates,"

and since the Mosaic Covenant says that, because of Israel's disobedience,

> "I will scatter you among the nations, and I will unsheathe the sword after you; and your land shall be a desolation, and your cities shall be a waste,"
>
> (Lev. 26:33)

both Covenants had to be honored by the faithful God who made them. The LORD honored the "Dual Covenants" first by dramatically sparing Jerusalem during the reigns of Jehoshaphat and Hezekiah according to the Abrahamic and Davidic Covenants, and then by enforcing the Mosaic

Covenant for a period of punishment and exile (and sab-baths for the Land), and in recent years enforcing anew the Abrahamic Covenant by starting to bring the Jews back to the Land of Israel. Even the Mosaic Covenant, after being broken by Israel, still demanded a restoration, as God promised in Deut. 30:4.

> "If your outcasts are in the uttermost parts of heaven, from there the LORD your God will gather you, and from there he will fetch you."

Therefore, Israel's punishment decreed by the Mosaic Covenant has now been completed; the blessings of the Abrahamic Covenant have just recently become more visible to the world. God is restoring his Chosen People to his Chosen Land in his Chosen Time. Only those Jews who persist in living in the Dispersion may still feel the remanent effects of the Mosaic Covenant's curses.

But back to ancient Judah and the frustrated prophet, Jeremiah. During Jeremiah's early days as a young prophet, the righteous King Josiah had been leading the nation in an exciting renewal of the Mosaic Covenant. Jeremiah had been thrilled to be a part of Josiah's renewal. Yet, within so few years God's People were again rejecting their vows during the reigns of three of King Josiah's evil sons, Jehoahaz, Jehoiakim and Zedekiah. And Jeremiah's message changed from revival to recrimination.

The New Covenant Predicted

Still, the angry God made yet another blessed promise. Even as the Babylonian soldiers were besieging the holy city,

God gave through Jeremiah one of the most exquisite prophecies in the Bible.

> "Behold, the days are coming, says the LORD, when I will make a new covenant with the house of Israel and the house of Judah, not like the covenant which I made with their fathers when I took them by the hand to bring them out of the land of Egypt, my covenant which they broke, though I was their husband, says the LORD. But this is the covenant which I will make with the house of Israel after those days, says the LORD: I will put my law within them, and I will write it upon their hearts; and I will be their God, and they shall be my people. And no longer shall each man teach his neighbor and each his brother, saying, 'Know the LORD,' for they shall all know me, from the least of them to the greatest, says the LORD; for I will forgive their iniquity, and I will remember their sin no more."   (Jer. 31:31-34)

Indeed, a most beautiful and important prophecy! Since his People had refused to honor the stipulations of the Mosaic Covenant, God declared, "I will make a *new* covenant with the house of Israel and the house of Judah."

As usual, the LORD spoke of the impending Covenant before actually establishing it, except that this time the predictions were made *centuries* ahead of the actual event. Jeremiah's exciting prophecy, hidden in the midst of all the woeful language of rebellion, apostasy and destruction, was to be one of the most crucial Old Testament scriptures for the early Christians, who were almost all Jewish. And somehow, this New Covenant was to be written "upon their hearts."

Other Old Testament prophets also spoke of such a future Covenant.

> "And I will make for you a covenant on that day with the beasts of the field, the birds of the air, and the creeping things of the ground; and I will abolish the bow, the sword, and war from the land; and I will make you lie down in safety. And I will betroth you to me for ever; I will betroth you to me in righteousness and in justice, in steadfast love, and in mercy. I will betroth you to me in faithfulness; and you shall know the LORD."
>
> (Hosea 2:18-20)

> "And as for me, this is my covenant with them, says the LORD: my Spirit which is upon you, and my words which I have put in your mouth, shall not depart out of your mouth, or out of the mouth of your children, or out of the mouth of your children's children, says the LORD, from this time forth and for evermore."   (Isaiah 59:21)

> "For this is like the days of Noah to me: as I swore that the waters of Noah should no more go over the earth, so I have sworn that I will not be angry with you and will not rebuke you. For the mountains may depart and the hills be removed, but my steadfast love shall not depart from you, and my covenant of peace shall not be removed, says the LORD, who has compassion on you."
>
> (Isa. 54:9,10)

> "I will make with them a covenant of peace and banish wild beasts from the land, so that they may

dwell securely in the wilderness and sleep in the woods. And I will make them and the places round about my hill a blessing; and I will send down the showers in their season; they shall be showers of blessing." (Ezek. 34:25,26)

"Behold, the days are coming," says the LORD, "when the plowman shall overtake the reaper and the treader of grapes him who sows the seed; the mountains shall drip sweet wine, and all the hills shall flow with it.

"I will restore the fortunes of my people Israel, and they shall rebuild the ruined cities and inhabit them; they shall plant vineyards and drink their wine, and they shall make gardens and eat their fruit. I will plant them upon their land, and they shall never again be plucked up out of the land which I have given them," says the LORD your God. (Amos 9:13-15)

"Thus says the LORD of hosts: Behold, I will save my people from the east country and from the west country; and I will bring them to dwell in the midst of Jerusalem; and they shall be my people and I will be their God, in faithfulness and in righteousness." (Zech. 8:7,8)

"At that time I will bring you home, at the time when I gather you together; yea, I will make you renowned and praised among all the peoples of the earth, when I restore your fortunes before your eyes," says the LORD. (Zephaniah 3:20)

It shall come to pass in the latter days that the mountain of the house of the LORD shall be established as the highest of the mountains, and shall be raised up above the hills; and peoples shall flow to it, and many nations shall come, and say: "Come, let us go up to the mountain of the LORD, to the house of the God of Jacob; that he may teach us his ways and we may walk in his paths." For out of Zion shall go forth the law, and the word of the LORD from Jerusalem.

He shall judge between many peoples, and shall decide for strong nations afar off; and they shall beat their swords into plowshares, and their spears into pruning hooks; nation shall not lift up sword against nation, neither shall they learn war any more; but they shall sit every man under his vine and under his fig tree, and none shall make them afraid; for the mouth of the LORD of hosts has spoken.   (Micah 4:1-4)

But these beautiful prophecies of a New Covenant were lost to the Jews who were bemoaning their cruel enslavement in Babylon. They were trying to figure out what had gone wrong with the unilateral covenants.

The prophets Jeremiah and Ezekiel—as the Babylonian Exile was beginning—explained God's logic. As Jeremiah expounded from Jerusalem, and Ezekiel from exile in Babylon, there was a *Dual* Covenant relationship between God and Israel. Although He had punished them severely, God was going to follow them in the Exile, remain with them and preserve them there—and bring them back at the appropriate time. This could be called "remnant theology." For their violation of the bilateral Covenant, God destroyed the majority, and He punished the remnant severely, all the while protecting that small group from extinction because of the covenants—both unilateral and bilateral.

The Dual Covenant relationship always preserves a significant remnant, which God in turn blesses, and his People multiply once again. Isaiah's earlier prophecy concerning the Assyrian loss of 185,000 soldiers had included such a "remnant" prediction, for the Land had already been ravaged by the Assyrians.

> "And this shall be the sign for you: this year you shall eat what grows of itself, and in the second year what springs of the same; then in the third year sow, and reap, and plant vineyards, and eat their fruit. And the surviving remnant of the house of Judah shall again take root downward, and bear fruit upward; for out of Jerusalem shall go forth a remnant, and out of Mount Zion a band of survivors. The zeal of the LORD will do this."
>
> (2 Kings 19:29-31)

Ezekiel's vision of the valley of dry bones (Ezekiel 37) is also a good prophetic example of remnant theology.

There have been several periods in human history during which the Jewish people were severely reduced in numbers, when God suddenly multiplied them. The nineteenth century was a dramatic modern example of an abrupt, unexplainable increase in the world Jewish population.

Remnant theology could not provide a complete answer to the paradox of the two contradictory covenant traditions, but it began to provide God's People with an intense hope for the future even while they suffered in exile.

"Behold, I will gather them from all the countries to which I drove them in my anger and my wrath and in great indignation; I will bring them back to this place, and I will make them dwell in safety. And they shall be my people, and I will be their God. I will give them one heart and one way, that they may fear me for ever, for their own good and the good of their children after them. I will make with them an everlasting covenant, that I will not turn away from doing good to them; and I will put the fear of me in their hearts, that they may not turn from me. I will rejoice in doing them good, and I will plant them in this land in faithfulness, with all my heart and all my soul."

(Jer. 32:37-41)

During their 40 to 60 years of Babylonian Captivity (three different groups of Jews were taken into exile during the years 597-581 B.C.), a lot of religious activity was occurring in their midst. To their surprise, the Jews discovered that God was in Babylon too. There the prophetic mantle fell upon a young man named Ezekiel. As his People had once esteemed the Abrahamic and Davidic Covenants so highly as the result of God's spectacular destruction of 185,000 Assyrian soldiers, so now, during the Babylonian Captivity, the Abrahamic-Davidic Covenants faded from their attention and the Mosaic Covenant became more prominent. After all, declared Ezekiel, it was the nation's violation of the Mosaic Covenant that had led to their current misery.

Following a generation of Jewish exile in Babylon, Cyrus the Persian, one of history's great benevolent dictators, conquered Babylon and promptly issued an edict that the Jews could go home. By this time, however, some Jews had become successful and comfortable in Babylon; they had learned how to prosper in Gentile lands, a skill that has never disappeared. So they returned only sporadically over succeeding centuries, the final exodus from the land of the Tigris and Euphrates Rivers having occurred as recently as our present generation.

"Covenant" Becomes "Law"

Among the prominent exiles to return to Jerusalem was a priest named Ezra. He was born in Babylon, and came to Judah perhaps at the insistence of the Jewish governor, Nehemiah, some 75 to 150 years after the first exiles returned. Ezra the priest appears to have thought along these lines: "If the Mosaic Covenant is so important to God that He would destroy our nation because of our violation of that Covenant, then we must organize Judah in such a manner that God could never again be so angry with his People. We *must* be a holy nation!"

So Ezra and his successors began to extrapolate rules from the Mosaic Covenant in great detail, expanding the Ten Commandments and their corollary expositions to a growing series of laws. "Law" was replacing "Covenant." The whole nation, under Ezra the priest and Nehemiah the governor, was being organized into a "holy" nation. The law was primarily religious, but it also affected all of secular life. It was a nationwide experiment in holiness. The priests emphasized circumcision, observance of the sabbath, strong family life, no intermarriage with foreigners, maintenance of the dietary laws, the abhorrence of all images in worship, the attending to the reading of scripture, and the organization of each Jewish community around a new teaching institution, the synagogue, along with the centralized system of worship and sacrifice in the rebuilt Temple in Jerusalem. Such was Jewish life from the fifth century B.C. onward. Covenant indeed had become Law.

For those who know Reformed church history, John Calvin organized Geneva, Switzerland, in the 1540's and 1550's along similar lines. Early Puritan Massachusetts was a similar experiment in "holiness by law." Community punishment for discovered violations could have been quite severe, not only in ancient Jerusalem, but also in Puritan New England. Sunday "blue laws" are a relic of such legislation.

The Jews after Ezra were truly a separate People, a nation set apart. They were usually under foreign domination, but the Jews were a proud People nonetheless. This was the Judaism into which Jesus of Nazareth was born.

By the time that strange "star" appeared over Bethlehem, Jewish thinkers had long been wondering, Whatever happened to the Davidic Covenant? David's descendants hadn't sat on the throne of Israel for more than 500 years. The Jews still enjoyed the high priestly line, but it too was destined to die out within several centuries. And the Abrahamic Covenant had apparently been broken too, for Jerusalem was subject to the hated Romans.

Each Passover the Jews ate the Pesach, reclining on the floor, as free men would eat; but the proud gesture had a hollow ring to it. The unilateral, unconditional covenants seemed to have only a nostalgia about them, and perhaps provided some limited basis for shallow ethnic boasting about what would happen to the Romans after the Messiah appeared. But where were the Promises? Where was God's deliverance? And, what in the world did Isaiah 53 mean? The Servant of the LORD in Isaiah 53 could not possibly be a *suffering* Servant! He is to be a victorious King! There were lots of confusing questions.

Another confusing question was to be found in Psalms 110. This is one of the "messianic" psalms, written for a king of Judah perhaps, but also looking ahead to the ideal King of the future. In the middle of Psalms 110 is found this perplexing line: "You are a priest for ever after the order of Melchizedek." Is the Messiah to be not only a King, but also a Priest? Many prophecies were quite difficult to sort out.

So the Jews made much of the Mosaic Covenant—"Torah," the Law. This they could understand.

Jewish people have always tended to be very much oriented to this world. Keeping earthly laws suited them well. Spiritual matters, heavenly concepts, eternal life, a future kingdom of God—all of these to this day tend to be foreign to most Jews. But not all Jews! A sizable minority at the time Jesus was born in Bethlehem was longing for and praying for that One who had been mentioned hopefully in a number of Old Testament prophecies, so many woven into covenant terminology. The following are some of the messianic prophecies.

> "Behold, the days are coming, says the LORD, when I will raise up for David a righteous Branch, and he shall reign as king and deal wisely, and shall execute justice and righteousness in the land. In his days Judah will be saved, and Israel will dwell securely. And this is the name by which he will be called: 'The LORD is our righteousness.' "
>
> (Jer. 23:5,6; see also 33:14-16)

There shall come forth a shoot from the stump of Jesse, and a branch shall grow out of his roots. And the Spirit of the LORD shall rest upon him, the spirit of wisdom and understanding, the spirit of counsel and might, the spirit of knowledge and the fear of the LORD. And his delight shall be in the fear of the LORD.

He shall not judge by what his eyes see, or decide by what his ears hear; but with righteousness he shall judge the poor, and decide with equity for the meek of the earth; and he shall smite the earth with the rod of his mouth, and with the breath of his lips he shall slay the wicked. Righteousness shall be the girdle of his waist, and faithfulness the girdle of his loins. (Isa. 11:1-5)

But you, O Bethlehem Ephrathah, who are little to be among the clans of Judah, from you shall come forth for me one who is to be ruler in Israel, whose origin is from of old, from ancient days.
(Micah 5:2)

The scepter shall not depart from Judah, nor the ruler's staff from between his feet, until he comes to whom it belongs; and to him shall be the obedience of the peoples. (Gen. 49:10)

(The *New American Standard Version* translates the third line—"until he comes to whom it belongs"—more literally: " . . . until Shiloh comes"; but the precise meaning is unclear. This verse has, however, traditionally been understood to be messianic).

"My servant David shall be king over them; and they shall all have one shepherd. They shall follow my ordinances and be careful to observe my statutes. They shall dwell in the land where your fathers dwelt that I gave to my servant Jacob; they and their children and their children's children shall dwell there for ever; and David my servant shall be their prince for ever. I will make a covenant of peace with them; it shall be an everlasting covenant with them; and I will bless them and multiply them, and will set my sanctuary in the midst of them for evermore. My dwelling place shall be with them; and I will be their God, and they shall be my people. Then the nations will know that I the LORD sanctify Israel, when my sanctuary is in the midst of them for evermore."

(Ezek. 37:24-28)

Rejoice greatly, O daughter of Zion! Shout aloud, O daughter of Jerusalem! Lo, your king comes to you; triumphant and victorious is he, humble and riding on an ass, on a colt the foal of an ass . . . As for you also, because of the blood of my covenant with you, I will set your captives free from the waterless pit. (Zech. 9:9,11)

Behold my servant, whom I uphold, my chosen, in whom my soul delights; I have put my Spirit upon him, he will bring forth justice to the nations. He will not cry or lift up his voice, or make it heard in the street; a bruised reed he will not break, and a dimly burning wick he will not quench; he will faithfully bring forth justice. He will not fail or be discouraged till he has established justice in the earth; and the coastlands wait for his law. (Isa. 42:1-4)

Messianic promises such as these may be found here and there throughout the Old Testament. So many of these glowing prophecies use specific covenant language. A growing groundswell of hope for the future, a visionary attitude, a restless idealism—these emotions were spreading abroad among the spiritually sensitive in Judaism. The concept of the Messiah was surfacing ever more prominently when Jesus was born in Bethlehem. Perhaps the Promises *were* still valid!

The Faithful Rechabites

Before we complete the Old Testament, our survey of unilateral, unconditional covenants would not be exhaustive without returning to an examination of Jeremiah 35. This is an interesting object lesson that God used for the Jerusalemites who were facing national destruction by the Babylonian army in 587 B.C. The Rechabites were a clan whose ancestor Jonadab, the son of Rechab, had forbidden his family to drink wine and commanded them to live in tents—for ever!

The LORD instructed Jeremiah to test the Rechabites by setting wine before them—nearly 300 years later—and Jonadab's descendants still refused to drink. The LORD's point was, Why can't my People obey Me as the Rechabites still obey their ancestor Jonadab?

Because of their faithfulness, God promised, "Jonadab the son of Rechab shall never lack a man to stand before me" (Jer. 35:19). Thus God made a commitment that Jonadab's male descendants would never die out. A minor unilateral covenant, to be sure, and it had no significant effect on biblical history, so far as we know. In fact, the word "covenant" does not even appear in that story. Nevertheless, it was just such a promise—an unconditional, unilateral covenant.

The most surprising aspect of the story is that the Rechabites were apparently from a nomadic tribe, dwelling all their generations in tents, as Jonadab had ordained, not even of the genealogy of Israel! They were aliens in the Land! In view of God's promise to the Rechabites, it could well be that the many nomadic people, still living in tents, wandering over the land of Israel today—non-Jewish people who have often been strongly supportive of Israel in their struggles against their Arab neighbors—are the direct descendants of Jonadab the Rechabite. This *appears* to be another of God's faithful promises.

The Holy Spirit Withdrawn

So many covenants! The conditional Mosaic Covenant with its many renewals throughout the Old Testament! The unilateral covenants—with Noah, with Abraham, with Phinehas and with David! And so many promises about a future *new* covenant!

How did all these covenants fit together? Did the "remnant theology" of Jeremiah and Ezekiel resolve the contradictions? Not really. Their explanation dealt only partially with the enigma of the unilateral and bilateral covenants. The Abrahamic and Davidic Covenants—apparently broken Covenants—remained unexplained. And yet, the Almighty God of all creation is able to take a number of contradictory components and fit them all together to solve logically-impossible puzzles. The resolution was yet to be provided in the dim but hopeful future.

It had been so long since Judah had had a prophet, indeed, centuries. Where was the Spirit of God?

> We do not see our signs; there is no longer any prophet, and there is none among us who knows how long. (Psalms 74:9)

> Thus there was great distress in Israel, such as had not been since the time that prophets ceased to appear among them. (1 Maccabees 9:27)

> And the Jews and their priests decided that Simon should be their leader and high priest for ever, until a trustworthy prophet should arise. (1 Maccabees 14:41)

The Roman boot was so heavy upon this proud nation. Some of the rabbis who sensed the air of expectancy were teaching that the People would know when the Messianic Age had dawned, because God would be sending prophets once again. That would mean the Holy Spirit had been returned. A perplexed rabbi must have shaken his head and ended many a theological discussion with these uncertain words: "We must wait for Elijah!" (Malachi 4:5).

God's people are so impatient! To God, "time" is quite different than it is to us.

> For a thousand years in thy sight are but as yesterday when it is past, or as a watch in the night. (Psalms 90:4)

> With the Lord one day is as a thousand years, and a thousand years as one day. (2 Peter 3:8)

Again and again Jewish patriots broke out in revolt against the Roman authorities, hoping to force God's hand in anticipation of his sending a military Messiah, but each rebellion ended in ignominious defeat and dispersal.

A peaceable, separatist religious group at Qumran, next to the Dead Sea, also took matters into their own hands. Adhering strongly to the Mosaic Covenant, the Qumran sect proclaimed itself to be the Community of the "new covenant" predicted by Jeremiah. It too ended in total disaster at the hands of the Roman army. The Qumran Community did inadvertently leave a precious heritage for us today— the Dead Sea Scrolls.

The last of the Jewish prophets had been Malachi, dating from the fifth century B.C. Malachi, in his brief prophecy, spoke of the biblical covenants a surprising number of times. The Old Testament ended with Malachi looking to the future.

> "Behold, I send my messenger to prepare the way before me, and the Lord whom you seek will suddenly come to his temple; the messenger of the covenant in whom you delight, behold, he is coming, says the LORD of hosts. But who can endure the day of his coming, and who can stand when he appears? . . .

> "For behold, the day comes, burning like an oven, when all the arrogant and all evildoers will be stubble; the day that comes shall burn them up, says the LORD of hosts, so that it will leave them neither root nor branch. But for you who fear my name the sun of righteousness shall rise, with healing in its wings . . .

"Behold, I will send you Elijah the prophet before the great and terrible day of the LORD comes."

(Mal. 3:1,2; 4:1,2,5)

The Holy Spirit Returned

And John the Baptist came on the scene, announcing the imminent coming of the One for Whom Israel had been waiting. The predicted "messenger"—in the spirit of Elijah—had arrived!

A prophet! After 500 dry years! The Gospel of Luke reports lots of sudden activity by the Holy Spirit. To a spiritually-perceptive Jew, the events surrounding the birth of John the Baptist and the birth of Jesus of Nazareth, as well as the prophecies of Simeon and Anna over the infant Jesus (Luke 1 and 2), would have demonstrated that the Messianic Age had indeed arrived. The Holy Spirit had been returned! God had begun to move in faithfulness to his covenants.

John the Baptist called the Jewish people to repentance, in preparation for the coming of Messiah. He spoke in terms that could be derived from the Mosaic Covenant.

For Herod had sent and seized John, and bound him in prison for the sake of Herodias, his brother Philip's wife; because he had married her. For John said to Herod, "It is not lawful for you to have your brother's wife." (Mark 6:17,18)

Quoting Lev. 18:16, John had proclaimed publicly that Herod had violated the Mosaic Covenant.

"You may not marry . . . your brother's wife, for
she is your brother's" (*TLB*).

Jesus of Nazareth also, as He preached and taught on the
Kingdom of God, continually called the Jewish people back
to the stipulations of the Mosaic Covenant. He especially
tangled with the religious lawyers who had diluted several
of the Commandments—and taught thus—in order to suit
their own purposes, particularly financial purposes.

"You are simply rejecting God's laws and tram-
pling them under your feet for the sake of tradition. For instance, Moses gave you this law from
God: 'Honor your father and mother.' And he said
that anyone who speaks against his father or
mother must die. But you say it is perfectly all right
for a man to disregard his needy parents, telling
them, 'Sorry, I can't help you! For I have given to
God what I could have given to you.' And so you
break the law of God in order to protect your man-
made tradition. And this is only one example.
There are many, many others."

(Mark 7:9-13, *TLB*)

Clearly, John the Baptist and Jesus of Nazareth both lived
and ministered as proper Jewish heirs of the Mosaic
Covenant.

As we noted, the Jewish religious teachers were often
proclaiming that God's People would know when the
Messianic Age was appearing, because the Holy Spirit would
be returned. Jesus seized an opportunity to point out the
fact that the Spirit of God *had been* returned, but the religious leaders were refusing to welcome or even recognize
Him.

One day, as he was teaching the people in the temple and preaching the gospel, the chief priests and the scribes with the elders came up and said to him, "Tell us by what authority you do these things, or who it is that gave you this authority." He answered them, "I also will ask you a question; now tell me, Was the baptism of John from heaven or from men?" And they discussed it with one another, saying, "If we say, 'From heaven,' he will say, 'Why did you not believe him?' But if we say, 'From men,' all the people will stone us; for they are convinced that John was a prophet." So they answered that they did not know whence it was. And Jesus said to them, "Neither will I tell you by what authority I do these things."

(Luke 10:1-8)

Jesus had a greater purpose in this incident than just needling his enemies. This was his point: If John the Baptist *was* a genuine prophet, then the Holy Spirit *has been* returned, *and* the Messianic Age is already here. That was the deeper meaning of Jesus' question, and we may be certain that the scribes perceived the message.

Jesus further took upon Himself the messianic title from the Book of Daniel, "the Son of man."

I saw in the night visions, and behold, with the clouds of heaven there came one like a son of man, and he came to the Ancient of Days and was presented before him. And to him was given dominion and glory and kingdom, that all peoples, nations, and languages should serve him; his dominion is an everlasting dominion, which shall

> not pass away, and his kingdom one that shall not
> be destroyed.   (Dan. 7:13,14)

And virtually everything Jesus taught could be found right
in the Jewish scriptures.

> "Think not that I have come to abolish the law
> and the prophets; I have come not to abolish them
> but to fulfil them. For truly, I say to you, till heaven
> and earth pass away, not an iota, not a dot, will
> pass from the law until all is accomplished."
>   (Matt. 5:17,18)

Many of the miracles the Old Testament prophets had done,
Jesus also did. Although the religious lawyers tried to catch
Him in error, his teachings were totally scriptural. In fact,
every doctrine in the New Testament can be found in the
Old Testament. Jesus also confirmed the universalism of the
Old Testament.

> "Truly, I say to you, not even in Israel have I found
> such faith. I tell you, many will come from east
> and west and sit at table with Abraham, Isaac, and
> Jacob in the kingdom of heaven, while the sons
> of the kingdom will be thrown into the outer dark-
> ness; there men will weep and gnash their teeth."
>   (Matt. 8:10-12)

III

The New Covenant

The Inauguration of the New Covenant

There was something electric about Jesus' final trip to Jerusalem. Excitement was running high, both among his disciples and the people in general. Many of them truly expected Jesus to seize a sword and initiate a war of liberation as a military, conquering Messiah. This is one of the reasons the chief priests, who could be considered to have been Roman puppets, were hostile to Jesus. As one of them complained,

> "If we let him go on thus, every one will believe in him, and the Romans will come and destroy both our holy place and our nation."
>
> (John 11:48)

The Romans could sense the unrest too. Jerusalem was always a tinderbox at Passover, waiting to explode in revolt; so the Roman garrison had been increased for the holiday. At least two of Jesus' disciples had been Zealots, revolutionaries who carried the short sword hidden within their robes. The chief priests thought they would frustrate another bloody revolt by eliminating this upstart Jesus of Nazareth. Nobody could understand Isaiah 53, the suffering Servant of God.

The Thursday evening dinner initiated that history-making weekend. Jesus' excited disciples had no idea that they were eating the sacrificial *meal* establishing the prophesied New Covenant, a New Covenant of salt.

> And he took bread, and when he had given thanks
> he broke it and gave it to them, saying, "This is
> my body which is given for you. Do this in remem-
> brance of me." And likewise the cup after supper,
> saying, "This cup which is poured out for you is
> the new covenant in my blood."
>
> (Luke 22:19,20)

Nor did his disciples, when they received the bread and the cup after dinner, understand that they were participating in the establishment of the *sign* of the New Covenant. Jesus' words, "new covenant in my blood," went right past them. Only later did the Holy Spirit bring it to their remembrance.

One more event—the primary event—remained to complete the inauguration of the New Covenant: the shedding of blood.

God had a precise schedule all planned. About midday on Friday, after the chief priests had seen Jesus securely nailed to the cross, his blood dripping to the earth, they smugly dusted off their hands and moved on to "more important matters."

Let's ask a controversial question. Who was responsible for the crucifixion of Jesus?

Certainly the crucifixion was at the heart of God's intentions. He had planned that Jesus would be "the Lamb slain from the foundation of the world" (Rev. 13:8). But we humans desire other humans to blame. Whom did God use to accomplish his plan?

Because of the Jewish mob who screamed for his blood, the Church has traditionally blamed the *Jews*. And there is some truth to that accusation. Jews, however, have protested that it was the *Romans* who killed the Lord. And there is some truth to this allegation also. In recent years many Protestant writers and speakers have declared that it was *our sins* that nailed Him to the cross. Surely there is truth in that statement. But the primary human responsibility must fall upon those who had religious authority—the chief priests and most (but not all) of the elders and lawyers.

Throughout the history of the Christian Church too, most (but again, not all) religious leaders have resisted every outpouring of God's Spirit. Entrenched leadership may say they desire revival, but their actions so often belie it. Renewal is normally squelched by "appointing a committee." Most of those in authority, whether in Judaism or in Christendom, enjoy the *status quo*, the prestige and the power. Revival "rocks the boat." Nothing has changed to this day. Religious leaders still seem to demand that God do things through them, their way. Those holding ecclesiastical power have always tended to be naturally hostile to spontaneous, Spirit-led revival. Jesus of Nazareth was perceived as a real threat to the religious *status quo*.

The chronology of Good Friday is suggested by the Gospel of John, that this particular Friday evening was the beginning of Passover (John 18:28). It was *the* holy day, a rare combination of the sabbath and Passover. After making certain that the troublemaker, Jesus of Nazareth, had been crucified, the chief priests and the people hastened back inside the city, anticipating the celebration of the annual Passover sacrifice in the magnificent Temple of Herod.

Having completed their ritual cleansings—as if they could wash Jesus' blood off their hands—the priests took a spotless lamb, specially chosen to be the Passover sacrifice, and laid it upon the altar. The huge throng of worshipers watched expectantly. To inaugurate the Passover, at precisely the ninth hour (3 p.m.), the high priest Caiaphas dramatically took a knife, and slit the throat of that spotless lamb.

In that very instant, outside the city wall, Jesus screamed with pain, and the spotless Lamb of God breathed his last. In the Temple, behind the bustling high priest, the veil of the Holy of Holies was ripped open, from top to bottom. God had instituted the New Covenant!

The Bilateral Covenant Fulfilled

Not only was the New Covenant now in effect, but also the "Old" Covenant, the Mosaic Covenant, the Law, was completed. Not abolished or overthrown, but completed, fulfilled, as Jesus said in the Sermon on the Mount.

> "Think not that I am come to destroy the law, or the prophets: I am not come to destroy, but to fulfill." (Matt. 5:17, *KJV*)

> For Christ [in his crucifixion and resurrection] is the end [full discharge] of the law [in its requirements]. (Romans 10:4)

The teachings of Jesus and the writings of Paul are so radically different from each other because Jesus ministered under the Mosaic Covenant, and He ministered almost exclusively among Jews. But, once Jesus' blood had been shed,

Paul then was called to minister under the New Covenant, and his ministry was primarily among Gentiles. Paul describes the order in Romans 15:8,9 (*TLB*).

> Remember that Jesus Christ came to show that God is true to his promises and to help the Jews. And remember that he came also that the Gentiles might be saved and give glory to God for his mercies to them. That is what the Psalmist means when he wrote: "I will praise you among the Gentiles, and sing to your name."

The Letter to the Hebrews includes several chapters that tell of what the Son of God's crucifixion and resurrection have done to the old sacrificial system. First, the author states the limitations of the Mosaic Covenant, that it

> . . . can never, by the same sacrifices which are continually offered year after year, make perfect those who draw near . . . For it is impossible that the blood of bulls and goats should take away sins . . . And every priest stands daily at his service, offering repeatedly the same sacrifices, which can never take away sins.
>
> (Hebrews 10:1,4,11)

But Jesus Christ

> . . . offered for all time a single sacrifice for sins . . . For by a single offering he has perfected for all time those who are sanctified . . . He [takes away] the first in order to establish the second.
>
> (Hebrews 10:12,14,9)

Now, says the author of Hebrews, the Temple sacrifices are meaningless, for " . . . there is no longer any offering for sin" (10:18).

> In speaking of a new covenant he treats the first
> as obsolete. And what is becoming obsolete and
> growing old is ready to vanish away.
>
> (Heb. 8:13)

Therefore, within a very few years, God allowed the Romans to destroy the massive Jerusalem Temple—permanently.

Man, perhaps not by necessity, but certainly by practicality, is going to sin. The sacrificial system attending the Mosaic Covenant was intended to deal with this problem on a continuing basis—covering sin with the blood of animals, but never totally removing it. The perfect Lamb of God shed *his* blood so that all who believe in Him could receive forgiveness once-and-for-all. When Jesus died on the cross, God the Enemy became God the Friend!

We call this act the Atonement—the most wonderful demonstration of God's grace—his undeserved mercy. We deserve hell, and He's given us heaven.

The New Covenant appeared to most Jews to be unacceptably radical, even though it had been repeatedly prophesied in the Old Testament. Those Jews who accepted Jesus as the Messiah could hardly use the word "covenant" without feeling uncomfortable. "Covenant" meant to them the Mosaic Law, and there were those Christians who were now declaring that the Law had been superseded. Of all the writers of the New Testament, only Paul and the author of Hebrews were able to use this special word meaningfully. Furthermore, "covenant" to their Roman overlords had illegal connotations; secret societies were banned in the Roman Empire.

But to the rest of the Jews! Particularly to those in authority, the message of the cross and its blessing for the entire human race were terribly offensive and scandalous. First, God had instituted the Mosaic sacrificial system among his Chosen People 1500 years before: How could the followers of this Jesus say it was now meaningless? Second, Christians were drifting away from the synagogue, away from the dietary laws, and, horrors! away from circumcision. And third, patriotic Jews would exclaim, "*We* are the Chosen People of God! Gentiles are accursed! The Gentiles were created by God only to provide fuel for the fires of hell!"

Those exclusivistic Jewish feelings were deep-seated, as we see when the Apostle Paul was mobbed in the Temple. Paul spoke to the Jewish crowd in Hebrew, and they listened quietly, until he said that Jesus had told him, "Depart; for I will send you far away to the Gentiles" (Acts 22:21). The crowd immediately went wild, demanding Paul's death. "Our God would *never* bless Gentiles!"

Even the leaders of the early Jerusalem Church were indignant over Peter's visit to Cornelius. "Why did you go to uncircumcised men and eat with them?" (Acts 11:4). If Cornelius and the others in his household hadn't received the Holy Spirit as a sovereign act of God, the Jerusalem Church leaders would never have accepted Peter's explanation. Further, it had to be God's sovereign act, for the very Jewish Peter would not have laid his hands upon those "unclean" Gentiles.

Patriotic Jews chose not to recognize the strong universal quality in the Abrahamic Covenant: "By you all the families of the earth shall bless themselves" (Gen. 12:3). Paul made much of this ecumenical thrust, describing it as "the plan of the mystery hidden for ages by God" (Eph. 3:9), "that is, how the Gentiles are fellow heirs, members of the same body, and partakers of the promise in Christ Jesus through the gospel" (Eph. 3:6).

Perhaps the most offensive statement (to a Jew) in the entire New Testament was 1 Peter 2:9,10.

> But you are a chosen race, a royal priesthood, a holy nation, God's own people, that you may declare the wonderful deeds of him who called you out of darkness into his marvelous light. Once you were no people but now you are God's people; once you had not received mercy but now you have received mercy.

These statements by Peter were a deliberate appropriation of God's Covenant-making words at Mt. Sinai, Exodus 19:5,6. *Twice* God took "no people" and made them "God's people." The Jews were indignant! "These Gentile Christians taking *our Covenant* and changing it so as to claim for themselves the blessings God has promised only to Jews!" No wonder the reaction was so often violent! The Jewish crowd in the Temple fully intended to kill Paul with their bare hands.

This scene demonstrates a strange phenomenon among God's People, whether Jewish or Christian. Those who are closest to God, who have been most blessed by his past works, are most apt to reject indignantly the very next outpouring of his blessings. This has been true throughout church history too. Perhaps that is why Jesus was talking about new wine being put into new wineskins (Mark 2:22). Sadly, the majority of the Jewish people, manipulated by their proud religious leaders, rejected the New Covenant that had been so beautifully promised by God through so many acknowledged prophets.

> He came to his own home, and his own people
> received him not.   (John 1:11)

All of us who are God's People typically create a picture in our minds of how God is supposed to act. If his Spirit behaves in a manner quite different from our personal desires and expectations, we tend to become suspicious and jealous, and often reject scornfully the Lord's spontaneous revivals. Strangely, God characteristically and historically pours out his Spirit upon those least esteemed by the religious "Establishment." He refuses to do things "our way." Therefore, those who once had the closest relationship with God usually overlook his very next renewal. The Rabbi Akiba (second century A.D.) complained in frustration, "Why does the Holy Spirit not come in power? We're doing everything we can to make Him feel welcome." The Spirit had already come, but the rabbi was willfully blinded to the Lord's Presence among the early Christians. Only when the "veil" is removed can a Jew perceive the truth (2 Cor. 3:14-16; 4:3,4).

Yet there is always that faithful minority among God's People, those who can recognize a genuine move of God because *He consistently acts scripturally.* Some of the Jews perceived the clear fulfillment of the Old Testament prophecies in Jesus of Nazareth. An enthusiastic, eloquent convert, Apollos,

> . . . powerfully confuted the Jews in public, show-
> ing by the scriptures that the Christ was Jesus.
>   (Acts 18:28)

In the early church "a great many of the priests were obedient to the faith" (Acts 6:7), and the Church at Jerusalem included some Pharisees (Acts 15:5). We may be sure that the presence of these priests and Pharisees greatly encouraged the rest of the Church.

Even then, those believing priests and Pharisees demanded the careful observance of the Law. "Unless you are circumcised according to the custom of Moses, you cannot be saved" (Acts 15:1). The Letter of James (and his speech in Acts 15) reveals the mediating position of one very Jewish elder of the Church. To suggest to these born-again priests and Pharisees, whose whole lives had been wrapped up in religious observances, that the entire basis of those observances was now meaningless—this was blasphemy! (See Acts 15:5.) Even though Jeremiah had clearly predicted its demise 600 years earlier, they could not bring themselves to believe that Jesus Christ, when He died on the cross, had fulfilled—and concluded—the Mosaic Covenant. The *only* bilateral, conditional Covenant between God and man had lasted 1500 years, and now it was completed. That was too painful a revelation! No wonder the Jerusalem Church died out after another generation-or-two!

The Apostle Paul agonized his way through this same revelation. Being a Pharisee himself, Paul had to endure Jesus' turning his theology upside down and shaking it out. But once the great Apostle heard from the Lord, and got his mind around what God had *really* accomplished in the New Covenant, he defended this Good News most eloquently.

Paul must have expended a great deal of time and effort in contrasting the Mosaic Covenant and the Abrahamic Covenant. His occasional preaching in the synagogues surely included much exposition on this very subject. It is no surprise that the reactions of the Jewish communities following Paul's sermons were quite animated in the least, and violent at times. The arguments would go on for hours, even days!

Paul's most thorough biblical exposition of the two Covenants (in his extant epistles) is found in Galatians, chapters 3 through 5. The Apostle was writing an angry letter to the churches of Galatia, a Roman province in central Asia Minor (modern Turkey). Paul had stopped there earlier because of an illness, and while in the area had won some converts to Jesus Christ.

The Galatian churches apparently were growing, until several of what are called "Judaizers" arrived. Judaizers were Jewish Christians "of the circumcision party," such as those who had indignantly protested (Acts 11) Peter's eating with Gentiles in Cornelius' house. These "super-Jews" were fiercely determined to weave together the bondage of the Mosaic Covenant with the freedom of the New Covenant, as they later demanded, "It is necessary to circumcise them [Gentile Christians], and to charge them to keep the law of Moses!" (Acts 15:5).

The Return of the Law

The visiting Judaizers enjoyed easy success in Galatia. These interlopers had only to open some scrolls of scripture for the Galatian Christians to read. There the Galatians found the Law, clearly written in apodictic (commandment) form, with the accompanying rules. "Paul gave you the truth about Jesus Christ," the Judaizers might have told them, "but Paul has a way of neglecting some important things in God's word."

Their speech was beguiling, to be sure. Soon the Galatian Christians were charmed into observing a number of traditional Jewish practices—circumcision, probably also the dietary laws, sabbath observance instead of the celebration of the Lord's Day, and Jewish holy days (Gal. 4:10).

Because Paul had been breaking up new ground in unevangelized areas, his early letters, such as 1 and 2 Thessalonians, show no evidence of Judaizing influences. So Paul was shocked and enraged when later he discovered what had been occurring in some of the churches *he* had organized! His Letter to the Galatians was scathing.

> O foolish Galatians! Who has bewitched you, before whose eyes Jesus Christ was publicly portrayed as crucified? Let me ask you only this: Did you receive the Spirit by works of the law, or by hearing with faith? Are you so foolish? Having begun with the Spirit, are you now ending with the flesh? Did you experience so many things in vain?—if it really is in vain. Does he who supplies the Spirit to you and works miracles among you do so by works of the law, or by hearing with faith? (Gal. 3:1-5)

Few people are able to write so eloquently when they are angry. Paul's five verses form perhaps the most powerful brief presentation ever written of the contrast between faith and law. Salvation—received by faith—can occur only with difficulty in a legalistic setting; miracles are rarely seen in a context of "law," as Paul emphasized so forcefully. The Holy Spirit tends to abandon legalistic churches. Religious people may feel comfortable with legalism, but the Spirit of God is quite uncomfortable there. Our only Old Testament hope is in the Abrahamic Covenant—the Promise; there is no hope in the Mosaic Covenant—the Law.

Since Paul was a minister "of a new covenant, not in a written code but in the Spirit, for the written [Mosaic] code kills, but the Spirit gives life'' (2 Cor. 3:6), he continued to illustrate his point in the Letter to the Galatians (chapters 3 and 4). The New Covenant in Jesus Christ is part of the fulfillment of the Promise to Abraham; it is the ending of the slavery of the Law of Moses. Paul painted an interesting allegory. Abraham had two sons, one by a slave woman (Hagar), representing the Covenant at Mt. Sinai, and corresponding to the Jerusalem of Paul's day, which, said the Apostle, is still in bondage. But the other son was the child of the free woman (Sarah), representing the Promise (the Abrahamic Covenant), and corresponding to the Jerusalem above (Revelation 21,22), which is free.

Paul was concerned that the Jews had so emphasized the Mosaic Covenant—the Law—that they seemed to have thought that God had annulled the Abrahamic Covenant— the Promise—superseding that earlier Covenant (Gal. 3:17). The Law, Paul said, was important to reveal the awfulness of sin, but the Promise to Abraham still remained valid through it all. Now that salvation through faith in Jesus Christ has come, the Law is no longer "our custodian." Rather, Jesus has set us free from the Law, that we might *all*—Jew and Gentile together—enjoy the blessings promised to Abraham on behalf of the whole world.

Paul emphasized this freedom from the Law that we Christians have in Christ, in the power of the Spirit (see also Col. 2:8-23; 1 Tim. 1:3-11), Characteristically—and tragically— God's People seem to gravitate, after a period of time, into legalism. There is a very human reason. It's idolatry! We want to be able to control our God. We all would like to ensure— by certain words, by certain forms or rituals, by certain "holy" behavior—the Presence of the Holy Spirit. Ironically, that's when He leaves!

One of the tragedies of church history is the attempt to *guarantee* the Presence of the Spirit of Christ by the use of the Eucharist. We have already discovered in the Book of Exodus that the manifestation of God cannot be assured by any physical representation, such as an image. Later the Jews tried to use circumcision, knowledge of God's personal Name (Yahweh), sabbath observance, the Temple, the Ark, etc., in order to guarantee the Presence and favor of God.

Unfortunately, the Christian Church has repeatedly, through the centuries, likewise tried to assure the attendance of the Holy Spirit by the manipulation of the Eucharist and related trappings. But the Spirit of God is a free Spirit (John 3:8); his Presence can never be guaranteed by any human act. He functions only upon his own initiative.

An altar too is unnecessary—yes, even counterproductive—in Christendom. An altar is a place of sacrifice for the purpose of appeasing a basically-hostile god, as in the Old Testament or in pagan rites. Under the New Covenant we need not appease God: his hostility has already been dealt with at the cross of Jesus, and God the Enemy has become God the Friend. Therefore, we cannot gain God's favor by anything we do—we already *have* his favor!

Worship has repeatedly become so overladen with "religion" that the Holy Spirit is actually made to feel uncomfortable. Perhaps, in the economy of God, it is time again for the fires of renewal to burn some of our idolatrous religious "furniture." As Shakespeare said,

> 'Tis mad idolatry
> to make the service greater than the god.
> —Troilus and Cressida (Act II, Scene 2, Line 56)

'Tis also an exercise in futility and, worse, it drives away the Spirit of God, to try to guarantee the Presence and blessing of God by any human ritual. Just as circumcision, dietary laws, etc., are now meaningless in gaining God's approval, so are the Church's religious trappings and precise formulas. Indeed, has not Jesus already told us that

> " . . . where two or three are gathered in my name, there am I in the midst of them!"
>
> (Matt. 18:20)

If we wish to guarantee Jesus' Presence, we can do it simply by gathering in his name. We cannot force the Lord to do anything He has already said He's going to do anyway! A special relationship with God is not assured by our use of sacraments; only God can initiate such a relationship, and He's already done it! We should celebrate the Lord's Supper in such a light.

> We have an altar from which those who serve the tent have no right to eat. (Hebrews 13:10)

Our "altar" is the Lord's Table, from which those who still offer sacrifices "have no right to eat." An altar is a place of sacrifice, but the once-for-all sacrifice has long since been offered. The Church, established in the blood of Jesus Christ, celebrates that two thousand-year-ago sacrifice each time it receives the Lord's Supper. We are no longer to remain in idolatrous bondage! We Christians *must* learn who we are through the blood of Jesus Christ!

Sacrifices under the New Covenant

Now that we have a New Covenant—unilateral, unconditional—what sacrifices *are* meaningful under that New Covenant?

We have noted earlier that most people seem to be somewhat uncomfortable in a relationship where they feel they "owe" something to God. The recipient of a gift has a continuing sense of obligation when the gift is unconditional. A sacrifice to God could make the worshiper feel he has done something—in turn—for God. Sacrifices were acceptable under the Mosaic Covenant; are there any acceptable sacrifices today?

Indeed, there are three sacrifices that are meaningful under the New Covenant. *First,* Romans 12:1,2 tells of one.

> I appeal to you therefore, brethren, by the mercies of God, to present your bodies as a living sacrifice, holy and acceptable to God, which is your spiritual worship. Do not be conformed to this world but be transformed by the renewal of your mind, that you may prove what is the will of God, what is good and acceptable and perfect.

Our bodies and our minds are to be given to God as sacrifices. Jesus has purchased us with his own blood (1 Cor. 6:19,20; 1 Peter 1:18,19). We are "a people for his possession" (1 Peter 2:9). Since He "owns" us, then we can freely live for Him, and the Lord will accept that sacrifice of ourselves and honor it by blessing us in countless ways. This gift to God is not something "outside" us by which we still maintain our self-will—money, food, good deeds—but the sacrifice is actually we ourselves! This is precisely what is meant by "making Jesus *Lord* of our lives." As the new Landlord, He is responsible for health, provision and protection.

The *second* New Covenant sacrifice is *praise.* Hebrews 12:28 and 13:15 tell of it.

> Therefore let us be grateful for receiving a king-
> dom that cannot be shaken, and thus let us offer
> to God acceptable worship, with reverence and
> awe . . . Through him then let us continually offer
> up a sacrifice of praise to God, that is, the fruit
> of lips that acknowledge his name.

Praise, worship, is an "acceptable" sacrifice. Spontaneous
praise by Christians elicits responses by the Holy Spirit
who dwells within us. The Spirit's reactions tend to be spontaneous also—varied, strengthening, sometimes surprising,
and filled with blessings that meet human needs.

All of us Christians would like to be assured of predictable behavior by the Spirit of God, but He remains a *free*
Spirit. Whenever we try to enclose the Holy Spirit in a
"box"—prescribed rituals, actions, words, prayers, etc.—He
is much less likely to honor our efforts. The Spirit of God
does respond enthusiastically whenever we worship the
Father and the Lord Jesus Christ, especially in our difficult
circumstances (Acts 4:31; 16:25,26). The biblical sacrifice
of praise—"the fruit of lips that acknowledge his name"—is
quite acceptable to God under the New Covenant. But it
must be emphasized again: We cannot guarantee any of the
Spirit's reactions to our praises.

A *third* form of acceptable sacrifice is pictured in Hebrews
13:16.

> Do not neglect to do good and to share what you
> have, for such sacrifices are pleasing to God.

1 John 3:17 describes this New Covenant sacrifice further.

> But if any one has the world's goods and sees his
> brother in need, yet closes his heart against him,
> how does God's love abide in him?

The author is speaking of Christians who are withholding from nearby, needy Christians, especially those within the same congregation. God expects such a sacrifice of sharing our worldly goods, and surely is disappointed when we do not care for one another within the local church.

> For we are his workmanship, created in Christ Jesus for good works, which God prepared beforehand, that we should walk in them. (Eph. 2:10)

But it must be repeated: None of these three sacrifices can win favor with God! We already *have* favor with God because of what Jesus Christ has done for us! Paul made that truth quite clear in the adjacent verses.

> For by grace you have been saved through faith; and this is not your own doing, it is the gift of God—not because of works, lest any man should boast.   (Eph. 2:8,9)

1 Peter 2:5 also speaks of sacrifices under the New Covenant in Jesus Christ.

> And like living stones be yourselves built into a spiritual house, to be a holy priesthood, to offer spiritual sacrifices acceptable to God through Jesus Christ.

Peter here appropriated the Mosaic Covenant concept, "a kingdom of priests," expanding it to include all believers in Jesus Christ. Peter continued: "But you [plural] are . . . a royal priesthood" (2:9). *All* Christians are priests called to offer proper sacrifices; not merely a select few chosen from the descendants of Aaron may minister before God. The veil of the Temple has been ripped in two, opening the way to God for every one of us.

Martin Luther seized upon this truth to proclaim "the priesthood of all believers." Together we form "a spiritual house"; "we are the temple of the living God" (2 Cor. 6:16). Whether alone or gathered, then, Peter says we are to "offer spiritual sacrifices acceptable to God through Jesus Christ." The sacrifices? They have already been named: we offer ourselves, our praises and our good works. These three sacrifices constitute our full priestly function before God.

Prophet and Priest

Some theologians have identified the four main figures (other than Jesus Christ) of both Testaments with particular covenant traditions. Abraham, of course, is identified with God's grace—the unilateral Promise; Moses with God's Law—the bilateral Covenant. In the New Testament, Paul is identified with grace—the unilateral Promise; and Peter with the bilateral Law.

Still another distinction may be made, this time between priest and prophet. The "priest" likes his religion orderly and predictable; the "prophet" is most comfortable with a God who is sometimes quite spontaneous, exciting and powerful. Moses (Old Testament) and Peter (New Testament) are to be identified with the priestly qualities, Abraham (Old Testament) and Paul (New Testament) with the prophetic.

Such differentiations are not totally valid; they serve only as general portrayals. Generally though, Peter may be perceived as a latter-day Moses, Paul as a latter-day Abraham.

Actually, we should observe a further distinction—between Christianity and "religion." Christianity is *not* a religion. One definition of religion is "man's efforts to find God, or, ascend toward God." In Christianity, God has come down to man in Jesus Christ—the exact opposite of religion. Religion is *evolutionary*; man must work to please his god or gods. Christianity (and Judaism, to some extent) is *revelational*; everything we know *about* God has been revealed to us *by* God, at his initiative. Therefore, every religion is merely that—religion. Christianity is Jesus!

An altar, as we have already noted, is a place for sacrifice, and thus is non-Christian (or pre-Christian at best). Since one who ministers at an altar is known as a priest, the office of priest is therefore hardly relevant to Christianity. Jesus Christ is Himself our High Priest for ever (Heb. 6:20); the once-for-all sacrifice has been made (Heb. 10:14); every Christian is a priest (1 Peter 2:5,9); so the ordained priest in Christendom today should be perceiving his role in terms of the New Testament office of pastor (Eph. 4:11).

New Covenant Stipulations?

Since God is the Superior Party to the New Covenant, are there *any* required stipulations for us Christians as the inferior party?

There is first the individual necessity to agree to the covenant. This presents a similarity to the Mosaic Covenant, in that the Israelites were asked if they were willing to accept the Covenant at Mt. Sinai.

> "If you will obey my voice and keep my covenant, you shall be my own possession among all

peoples; for all the earth is mine, and you shall
be to me a kingdom of priests and a holy nation."
(Exodus 19:5,6)

But the greater similarity to the New Covenant is found,
again, in the Abrahamic Covenant, where Abram "believed
the Lord; and He reckoned it to him as righteousness" (Gen.
15:6). Faith was the key to Abraham's reception of the
Covenant of Promise, and faith is also the key to our acceptance of the New Covenant in Jesus Christ. With the New
Covenant, man's agreement is spelled out in Romans 10:9.

> If you confess with your lips that Jesus is Lord and
> believe in your heart that God raised him from the
> dead, you will be saved.

A most obvious difference from Exodus 19:5,6—the
acceptance of the Mosaic Covenant—is that agreement to
the New Covenant is not national, but individual and personal. Jeremiah and Ezekiel predicted this individualism also,
as the latter prophesied,

> "What do you mean by repeating this proverb con-
> cerning the land of Israel, 'The fathers have eaten
> sour grapes, and the children's teeth are set on
> edge'? As I live, says the Lord GOD, this proverb
> shall no more be used by you in Israel. Behold,
> all souls are mine; the soul of the father as well
> as the soul of the son is mine: the soul that sins
> shall die.

> "If a man is righteous and does what is lawful and
> right—if he does not eat upon the mountains or
> lift up his eyes to the idols of the house of Israel,

does not defile his neighbor's wife or approach
a woman in her time of impurity, does not oppress
any one, but restores to the debtor his pledge, commits no robbery, gives his bread to the hungry and
covers the naked with a garment, does not lend
at interest or take any increase, withholds his hand
from iniquity, executes true justice between man
and man, walks in my statutes, and is careful to
observe my ordinances—he is righteous, he shall
surely live, says the Lord GOD."

(Ezekiel 18:2-9)

No longer, said God through the prophet, will I judge whole
nations, but rather individuals. Each man will be responsible to Me for himself.

There is, however, one vital qualification of this
doctrine—the Jewish People. Through the centuries,
innumerable thousands of Jews have accepted Jesus as the
Messiah, but always as individuals, like everyone else. These
Jews sooner or later become amalgamated into Christendom,
each one receiving the full blessings of the New Covenant.
Still, God treats the unbelieving Jews as a distinct nation,
his Chosen People. And, in God's perfect timing, He will
once again deal with this People "for his name's sake," for
the sake of his promises to Abraham, Isaac and Jacob. We
will investigate the matter at a later time.

We noted earlier that the Second Commandment was a
freeing Commandment. Under the Mosaic Covenant, Israel
no longer was to be concerned with appeasing the principalities and powers of this world. Likewise, accepting Jesus
Christ as Lord provides an even greater freedom under the
New Covenant. When Jesus is Lord of their lives, Christians
discover they are not alone, and that the Spirit of Jesus
provides a very personal strength, care, encouragement,

guidance, protection and healing. He intends to *free* Christians from many worldly concerns, as well as from demonic oppression, enabling us to live in freedom and in victory. "Jesus is Lord!" is our key.

But are there any other stipulations, any ordinances required of Christians?

There are indeed some specific instructions under the New Covenant. We are to " . . . go into all the world and preach the gospel to the whole creation" (Mark 16:15). We are to "love one another" (John 13:34). We are to wash one another's feet (John 13:14-17). We are to greet one another with the holy kiss (1 Cor. 16:20; 2 Cor. 13:12; 1 Thes. 5:26). We are to anoint and pray for the sick for healing (James 5:13-16). Such instructions (and others) are urged upon us.

But the New Covenant is operative whether or not we follow these stipulations. "Him who comes to me I will not cast out" (John 6:37). God has bound Himself; the blessings of the New Covenant are permanent, irrevocable, unbreakable. Only man can reject them. For the Superior Party once again—at the cross— humbled and bound Himself before the inferior party.

Perhaps an individual Christian is not very loving toward some of his brethren, ignoring the Love Commandment of Jesus: "A new commandment I give to you, that you love one another" (John 13:34). We are reminded of God's commandment to Abraham: "Walk before me, and be blameless"—a commandment, true; but the Covenant was operative whether or not Abraham remained "blameless." The New Covenant too remains in force, whether or not a Christian obeys the Love Commandment. Disobedient Christians simply miss a lot of the blessings God desires for us in this life.

"Salvation" is the New Testament word which describes all that Jesus has gained for us in his death and resurrection. According to the word's precise usages in the New Testament, the benefits of salvation include all of these: eternal life, physical healing, deliverance from evil spirits, and protection from danger or premature death. We Christians must learn all that is ours. God has already *obligated* Himself to provide these blessings under the New Covenant. Christians—those who have been "saved" from sin—are entitled to all of the blessings; what we receive is limited only by our lack of faith in God's promises. God does not limit his Gift to us ("It is not by measure that He gives the Spirit," John 3:34). Our problem is not accepting all of salvation that the Atonement has purchased. Jesus made a most challenging statement about faith.

> "Truly, I say to you, whoever says to this mountain, 'Be taken up and cast into the sea,' and does not doubt in his heart, but believes that what he says will come to pass, it will be done for him. Therefore I tell you, whatever you ask in prayer, believe that you have received it, and it will be yours."   (Mark 11:23,24)

The Family of God

There were a few mentions in the Old Testament of one special truth, that God is a Father to his earthly children. Again, Malachi, the final prophetic book of the Old Testament, used such language. "If then I am a Father, where is my honor?" (1:6). "Have we not all one Father? Has not one

God created us?'' (2:10). Several psalms and prophetic statements had earlier referred to God as Father.

> Father of the fatherless and protector of widows
> is God in his holy habitation.   (Psalms 68:5)

> "He shall cry to me, 'Thou art my Father.'"
> (Psalms 89:26)

> For thou art my Father, though Abraham does not
> know us and Israel does not acknowledge us;
> thou, O Lord, art our Father, our Redeemer from
> of old is thy name.   (Isa. 63:16)

> Yet, O Lord, thou art our Father.   (Isa. 64:8)

> "My Father, thou art the friend of my youth."
> (Jer. 3:4)

> "And I thought you would call me, My Father, and
> would not turn from following me."   (Jer. 3:19)

> "For I am a Father to Israel."   (Jer. 31:9)

So, when Jesus consistently spoke of God as his Father, and
taught his disciples to pray, saying, "Our Father," He was
not giving out a new teaching, although the authorities
wanted to kill him for it.

> This was why the Jews sought all the more to kill
> him, because he not only broke the sabbath but
> also called God his own Father, making himself
> equal with God.   (John 5:18)

Jesus was teaching his followers about the personality of their God who would be making a new covenant with them. He might well have spoken to his disciples at the Last Supper: "I am personally making peace with God for you, so no longer will He be known as a God who terrifies. He is your heavenly Father! And just as an earthly father makes a unilateral, unconditional covenant with his children, so—because of my blood—your heavenly Father will be making such a covenant with you."

As we noted early in our study, the parent-child relationship is the only earthly covenant that is unconditional, so we see in it the model for God's New Covenant in Jesus Christ. He is our heavenly Father, and even if we must be disciplined as children for our disobedience, He still loves us. "He disciplines us for our good, that we may share his holiness" (Hebrews 12:10).

The whole structure of New Covenant relationships is modelled after the ideal human family; Christians are all part of the Family of God. As our loving heavenly Father, He instructs his children to "love one another," binding the Family together in a firm and lasting blood-covenant relationship. That ancient critic of Christianity, Celsus, in his attempted slur upon Christians, was quite properly commending us when he sneered, "These Christians love each other even before they are acquainted!"

An illustration of this Family relationship is found in Paul's warning in 1 Cor. 11:27-30.

> Whoever, therefore, eats the bread or drinks the cup of the Lord in an unworthy manner will be guilty of profaning the body and blood of the Lord. Let a man examine himself, and so eat of the bread and drink of the cup. For any one who eats and drinks without discerning the body eats

and drinks judgment upon himself. That is why many of you are weak and ill, and some have died.

"The body" to be discerned could have two meanings. First, there is the physical body of Jesus who died on the cross. Second, there is the Church, which is also "the body of Christ." Which body did Paul mean?

Paul intended that we discern *both* bodies, leading to his emphasis upon the second: " . . . the church, which is his body." (Eph. 1:23). Using the human family as a type of the Church, when a wife and mother commits adultery, her act has a devastating effect upon her earthly family. When a husband and father abandons his wife and children, like-wise is the family unit shattered. A son or daughter who, in anger, walks out of the home, never to return, causes a breaking up of that family. So a church member, receiving the Communion without repenting of his bitterness toward certain of the brethren, invites division into the church family and increased exposure to sickness and premature death for himself. A close-knit, loving congregation will always enjoy significantly better health.

A continuing joy and blessing of living together under the New Covenant is not only that the blood of Jesus has cleansed us from all our past sin. There is also the *enduring* efficacy of his cleansing blood.

If we walk in the light, as he is in the light, we have fellowship with one another, and the blood of Jesus his Son cleanses us from all sin . . . If we confess our sins, he is faithful and just, and will forgive our sins and cleanse us from all unrighteousness. (1 John 1:7,9)

This letter was written to Christians. Thus, daily sins, because of this promise to the Church, may be forgiven following repentance. We may therefore enjoy the daily joy of walking confidently, in freedom, as the result of the blood of the New Covenant. Hebrews 10:29 describes in fearful language what might happen to a Christian who deliberately denies and ridicules the Covenant relationship after having accepted adoption into the Family.

> How much worse punishment do you think will be deserved by the man who has spurned the Son of God, and profaned the blood of the covenant by which he was sanctified, and outraged the Spirit of grace?

This ominous scripture causes us to wonder if the Ten Commandments hold any efficacy today, now that the Mosaic Covenant is fulfilled. Is the "Law" still meaningful—in spite of our demonstration that it has now been set aside?

Yes, the Ten Commandments are still quite valid, but in a new way. Paul relates them to the Love Commandment.

> Owe no man anything, except to love one another; for he who loves his neighbor has fulfilled the law. The commandments, "You shall not commit adultery, You shall not kill, You shall not steal, You shall not covet," and any other commandment, are summed up in this sentence, "You shall love your neighbor as yourself." Love does no wrong to a neighbor; therefore love is the fulfilling of the law.
> (Romans 13:8-10)

Love will not violate any of the Ten Commandments. The Commandments are not to be set aside, allowing a license to sin in the name of "love." Love fulfills the Commandments, and goes beyond. When love causes us to go the second mile, doing more than is required, then the Law is no longer a chain, clanking along our path, reminding us of its bondage. Love is aggressive, looking beyond the rules for opportunities to serve.

We could use "the tithe" as an analogy to the bondage of the Law versus the freedom of the Love Commandment. The giving of one's tithe—even if done mechanically—establishes the base for a Christian's financial freedom. While the 10% share for the Lord is from the earlier Patriarchs, Abraham and Jacob, the Mosaic Covenant confirms it rather legalistically. So, if the tithe seems a legalism, the creative Christian will give *11% or more* of his income to the Lord's work. That's how the Love Commandment operates too. The loving Christian seeks ways to do more than is required. Only those Christians who live in such freedom can understand this truth.

> "And you will know the truth, and the truth will make you free . . . So if the Son makes you free, you will be free indeed."   (John 8:32,36)

Old Testament Types in the New Covenant

God purposely established the New Covenant according to the pattern of the Old Testament covenants. First came its prediction, found many times in the Old Testament. Second was the sacrificial meal, commonly called the Last Supper, which continued to be commemorated as the "Love Feast" in the early Church (see Jude 12), but is today practiced by only a minority of Protestant churches. This was followed by the sign of the New Covenant, the bread and the cup, as is currently celebrated in nearly every Christian church. Then occurred the shedding of his blood by the Lord Jesus Christ, which constituted the Covenant's formal establishment. We Christians then ratify the New Covenant individually when we accept Jesus as Lord of our lives. And we continue to acknowledge the Covenant's blessings each time we receive the Eucharist.

There is yet another sign of the New Covenant. Baptism—from the Greek *baptizo*, meaning immersion in water—symbolizes the believer's death to sin and resurrection to new life in Jesus Christ.

Baptism is linked to three Old Testament signs, all involving covenants. 1 Peter 3:20,21 tells of

> . . . the days of Noah, during the building of the ark, in which a few, that is, eight persons, were saved through water. Baptism, which corresponds to this, now saves you, not as a removal of dirt from the body but as an appeal to God for a clear conscience, through the resurrection of Jesus Christ.

Baptism is likened to Noah's experience with the waters, which meant death to the world while Noah and his family survived. Peter stated that baptism is "an appeal to God." However, the original Greek word for "appeal" is stronger. It actually has the sense of "pledge" or "covenant," linking Christian baptism directly to a very personal acceptance of the New Covenant in Jesus Christ. This is why many churches reject infant baptism, requiring "believers' baptism."

Baptism is also compared to the sign of the Abrahamic Covenant in Col. 2:11-13.

> In him also you were circumcised with a circumcision made without hands, by putting off the body of flesh in the circumcision of Christ; and you were buried with him in baptism, in which you were also raised with him through faith in the working of God, who raised him from the dead. And you, who were dead in trespasses and the uncircumcision of your flesh, God made alive together with him, having forgiven us all our trespasses.

The comparison of baptism with circumcision is most fitting. The New Covenant is largely an expansion of the Abrahamic Covenant, which had circumcision as its sign.

A third Old Testament type of Christian baptism is found in 1 Cor. 10:1,2.

> I want you to know, brethren, that our fathers were all under the cloud, and all passed through the sea, and all were baptized into Moses in the cloud and in the sea.

Just as the Red Sea formed the waters from which ancient Israel was saved, so the baptismal waters are a sign for the Christian of a washing from sin, a separation from the world, and a salvation from death and eternal punishment.

Thus we find three Old Testament covenant types foreshadowing the New Testament baptism in water—Noahic, Abrahamic and Mosaic. Two of them deal appropriately with salvation from death by water for God's Chosen Ones. However, Christian baptism is not itself the "death" to sin; to the repentant new Christian it is, rather, the "funeral service" for the sinful man who has already died.

A careful study of modern church history reveals an interesting bit of information about God's view of Christian baptism. Regardless of whether water baptism is adult or infant, by immersion, pouring or sprinkling, in Jesus' name or in the name of the Father, Son and Holy Spirit, or even no water baptism at all—the Spirit of God refuses to honor a legalistic approach to Christian baptism. *Faith* is still the key that moves the Holy Spirit, although Christians who have had a profound spiritual experience with Jesus Christ often spontaneously request adult, immersion baptism if they have not already been so baptized. This is the work of the Spirit of God in their hearts.

The Gift of the Holy Spirit

The New Covenant provides us with still more blessings. We note another key difference between the "Old" Covenant and the New Covenant. In the Old Testament the Holy Spirit was given only to certain favored persons, sovereignly chosen by God—Moses, Bezalel, Joshua, the judges, Samuel and the prophets who followed. Then, some time after the return from the Exile, the Spirit of God was withdrawn for about five centuries. Finally, under the terms of the New Covenant, "every one whom the Lord our God calls to Him" may receive the Holy Spirit.

In the very moment Peter the Jew spoke that fateful word "whosoever" to Cornelius the Gentile, the Holy Spirit fell on all the Gentiles in the house (Acts 10:43,44).

Therein lies the primary difference between life in the Old Testament community and life in the New Testament community. It's "whosoever." We may *all* receive the Spirit. Jeremiah predicted it.

> "I will put my law within them, and I will write
> it upon their hearts . . . And no longer shall each
> man teach his neighbor and each his brother, say-
> ing, 'Know the LORD,' for they shall all know me,
> from the least of them to the greatest."
> (Jer. 31:33-34)

The Mosaic Covenant was written on stone (Exodus 34:1),
but the New Covenant in Jesus Christ is written on human
hearts.

> You are a letter from Christ delivered by us, writ-
> ten not with ink but with the Spirit of the living
> God, not on tablets of stone but on tablets of
> human hearts.   (2 Cor. 3:3)

It is the Spirit of God who writes God's law; and because
He dwells within the heart of every believer, He writes God's
law upon the heart, or in the spirit, of that believer.

Philippians 2:13 explains the effect of the Holy Spirit upon
the Christian within whom He dwells.

> For God is at work within you, helping you want
> to obey Him, and then helping you do what He
> wants (*TLB*).

This verse sums up the practical outworking—in the present age—of God's intended life under the New Covenant,
as predicted by Jeremiah. First, the Holy Spirit, working in
our spirits, causes us to "want to obey" God; then He
empowers us to accomplish supernaturally "what He wants."
The Holy Spirit is the Key. The Holy Spirit:

(1) is described by his Greek name, Paraclete—
Comforter, Counselor, Helper, Befriender;
(John 14:16,26)
(2) convinces of sin;   (John 16:8)
(3) gives new birth;   (John 3:5; 6:63)
(4) cleanses;
(Romans 15:16; 1 Cor. 6:11; Titus 3:5)
(5) teaches;   (John 14:26)
(6) guides into all the truth;
(John 16:13; 1 John 2:20,27)
(7) explains the scriptures;   (Luke 24:45)
(8) searches everything;   (1 Cor. 2:10)
(9) bears witness to Jesus;   (John 15:26)
(10) declares the things to come; (John 16:13)
(11) gives visions and prophecies;
(Luke 2:25,27; Acts 20:23; Rev. 1:1,10; 2:7)
(12) gives spiritual gifts;
(1 Cor. 12:4-11; Hebrews 2:4; 1 Peter 4:10)
(13) gives utterance in other tongues;
(Acts 2:4; 10:44-46; 19:1-6)
(14) enables believers to pray and sing in the
Spirit;   (1 Cor. 14:15; Eph. 6:18; Jude 20)
(15) enables believers to discern the signs of the
times;   (Matt. 16:1-4; 1 Tim. 4:1-3)
(16) fills those who ask for Him;
(Luke 11:10-13; Acts 2:38)
(17) gives power to witness for Jesus;
(Matt. 10:20; Mark 13:11; Acts 1:8; 4:8-12,31)
(18) confirms by signs the words of those who
witness for Jesus;   (Mark 16:20)
(19) enables believers to conduct successful
evangelism;   (Romans 15:18,19)
(20) causes believers to want to obey God;
(Phil. 2:13)

(21) enables believers to do greater works than Jesus did; (John 14:12)

(22) gives power over Satan;
(Matt. 12:29; Acts 13:11; 16:18; 2 Cor. 10:4; 1 John 4:4)

(23) produces "fruit" in believers;
(Gal. 5:22,23)

(24) inspired the writing of scripture;
(2 Tim. 3:16,17)

(25) enables believers to heal the sick;
(Luke 4:40; Acts 10:38)

(26) empowers believers to cast out demons;
(Matt. 12:28; Luke 11:20)

(27) helps believers in their weakness, interceding for the saints; (Romans 8:26,27)

(28) prepares the way for the coming of Jesus;
(Joel 2:28,29; Eph. 5:26,27; Rev. 22:17)

Although He causes us to want to obey God, the Holy Spirit will not force us to do his will. He never stops us from sinning; but He certainly keeps us from enjoying our sin!

We are reminded again of Jeremiah's prophecy of the new covenant to come: "I will put my law within them, and I will write it upon their hearts" (31:33). When God Himself dwells within us, walking obediently in his Covenant is not difficult; indeed, He makes it enjoyable. The Holy Spirit, who will fill every believer who asks for Him, takes us into the unexpected, the thrilling, the "impossible":

Now glory be to God who by his mighty power at work within us is able to do far more than we would ever dare to ask or even dream of— infinitely beyond our highest prayers, desires, thoughts, or hopes. (Eph. 3:20, *TLB*)

God the Father is able to do, and is desirous of doing, more than we would ever dream of—by the Power who actually dwells *within* each Spirit-filled Christian. The very thought is awesome!

Phil. 2:13 and Eph. 3:20 are both remarkable scriptures, indicating the amazing power of the Holy Spirit—dwelling within us!

> For God is at work within you, helping you want to obey Him, and then helping you do what He wants (*TLB*).

> Now glory be to God who by his mighty power at work within us is able to do far more than we would ever dare to ask or even dream of— infinitely beyond our highest prayers, desires, thoughts, or hopes (*TLB*).

These statements make it obvious that all of us Christians are living and serving far below the levels God desires us to reach by the Power Whom He has placed within us. Surely our God is disappointed; but the New Covenant in Jesus Christ is an unconditional Covenant, so the Lord continues to bless his Church, faithful or not. To think that Almighty God would entrust each of us with his very own Spirit!

If God's People could only comprehend his incredible trust in us—we who are imperfect at our best and disgusting at our worst—the Church of Jesus Christ would accomplish the Great Commission in this generation! Knowing all these great truths, Christians should stand much taller, walk with much more poise, and serve with much more confidence.

The Unconditional Covenants Today

Now, what about each of the unilateral, unconditional Old Testament Covenants? Do they possess validity today?

(1) The Noahic Covenant still stands, its promise to the whole human race as valid as ever. God will allow the earth to be destroyed by *fire* some day, but never again by water.

(2) The Abrahamic Covenant, designated by Paul as "the Promise," is especially viable. Jesus Christ is responsible for its flowering, coming into fuller bloom as an eternal Covenant. "By your descendants shall all the nations of the earth bless themselves" (Gen. 22:18). "All the nations of the earth" have already blessed themselves so much by the Promise, but the gracious effects of this Covenant upon the world will be seen to an even greater degree in the near future.

(3) The Levitical Covenant has also blossomed in Jesus Christ, for He has "become a high priest for ever" (Hebrews 6:20). To the Jew who was troubled by the dying out of the earthly line of high priests, Jesus is the Answer. Jesus Christ is our High Priest for ever, continually interceding with the Father for us all (1 John 2:1).

(4) The Davidic Covenant too has come into its fullness in Jesus Christ, for He is in the direct earthly lineage of David, and He is King of kings and Lord of lords. "Of this man's [David's] posterity God has brought to Israel a Savior, Jesus, as he promised" (Acts 13:23). "The Lion of the tribe of Judah, the Root of David, has conquered" (Rev. 5:5). Here too is the answer to the Jew who questioned the apparent end of the Davidic dynasty. David's inheritance is indeed eternal (Psalms 89:28,29).

Jews who may have wondered also about Psalms 110, the messianic psalm, linking the eternal priesthood with the eternal kingship, will find that answer also in Jesus Christ.

"You are a priest for ever, after the order of Melchizedek" (110:4). Hebrews 5 through 7 discusses this point. Jesus Christ is High Priest for ever, and He is also King of kings for ever. The union of the Levitical and the Davidic Covenants is complete in Him eternally.

A fascinating 500-year calendar dates the unilateral covenants. According to biblical dating, these five covenants are spaced (rather roughly) 500 years apart: Noahic—2500 B.C.; Abrahamic—2000 B.C.; Levitical—1500 B.C.; Davidic—1000 B.C.; Jeremiah's and Ezekiel's predictions of the New Covenant—500 B.C.; the New Covenant in Jesus Christ—Zero B.C./A.D.

The Chosen People in the Chosen Land

Returning to the second century A.D., now we have the answers for Justin Martyr's Jewish debating opponent, Trypho. Now we have responded to Celsus' unnamed Jew, with his bitter criticisms of Christianity. Modern Jews seldom know the Old Testament; but when they do know their scriptures, this book will make sense to them. As in the Apostle Paul's day, the two basic Old Testament scriptures that should be pointed out to Jews who truly love God are Isaiah 53 and Jer. 31: 31-34. The Holy Spirit will bring these prophecies to life in their hearts.

> "I ask, then, has God rejected his people? By no means! . . . God has not rejected his people whom he foreknew." (Rom. 11:1,2)

For the Jews remain God's very special "Covenant People," not because of their faithfulness, but because of God's personal commitment in the Abrahamic Covenant. "It is not for your sake, O house of Israel, that I am about to act, but for the sake of my holy name" (Ezek. 36:22). God's name *will be* honored and his credibility *will be* acknowledged!

And so, God isn't finished yet with his blessings for the Chosen People. Not in the least has He forgotten them! The Abrahamic Covenant continues to work on behalf of the Jews. In fact, the modern world has just begun to see what the Abrahamic Covenant means for Israel. Paul has spoken to this point in Romans 11.

Paul first described the place of Gentile Christians here on earth. Gentile believers, said Paul, have been grafted into the olive tree (Israel is sometimes symbolized by the olive tree in scripture), so the Gentiles also have inherited the blessings of Abraham. This is the mystery plan hidden for ages by God (Eph. 2:11-3:12). Gentile Christians are the "New Israel," *not replacing* the "Old Israel," but grafted into the original olive tree, adopted into the Family of God. This is the clear biblical truth that many Christian scholars such as Augustine have failed to grasp.

But what about those Jews who continue to reject Jesus Christ, the Son of God? Do they have a future? Paul predicted in Romans 11 how the Abrahamic Covenant will once again bless them at the end of the age.

> And even the [Jews], if they do not persist in their unbelief, will be grafted in, for God has the power to graft them in again. For if you have been cut from what is by nature a wild olive tree, and grafted, contrary to nature, into a cultivated olive tree, how much more will these natural branches be grafted back into their own olive tree.

Lest you be wise in your own conceits, I want you
to understand this mystery, brethren: a hardening
has come upon part of Israel, until the full number of the Gentiles come in, and so *all Israel will
be saved*; as it is written,

"The Deliverer will come from Zion,
he will banish ungodliness from Jacob";
"and this will be my covenant with them
when I take away their sins."

As regards the gospel they are enemies of God, for
your sake; but as regards election they are beloved
for the sake of their forefathers. For the gifts and
the call of God are irrevocable.

(Romans 11:23-29)

Paul was predicting—and fully expecting—a mighty move
of God's Spirit among the unbelieving Jewish People some
day. That day is yet to come. Perhaps we could say it is just
beginning. At that point in God's time when "the full
number of the Gentiles [has] come in, . . . all Israel will be
saved" also. Luke 21:24 is quite suggestive.

"Jerusalem will be trodden down by the Gentiles,
until the times of the Gentiles are fulfilled" (See
also Rev. 11:2).

"The times of the Gentiles" are apparently fulfilled, since
Jerusalem has been under Israeli control for more than 20
years.

Liberal scholars have long considered these statements
about the salvation of the Jews in Romans 11 to be merely
Paul's wishful thinking. But liberals can hardly recognize
God's hand working in contemporary human history. There

are countless Old Testament scriptures telling, in agreement with the Apostle Paul, of such glorious things that God will do for his Chosen People "in the latter days." The Lord will not be prevented from accomplishing a single promise concerning Israel, for each one has its basis in the *unbreakable* Abrahamic Covenant. The international stage is almost set for the supernatural fulfillment of the remainder of this prophecy. The Church should be praying for it.

The Unity of the Scriptures

Perhaps the reader has already observed that the search for the biblical covenants includes reference to nearly all of the 66 books of the Bible, excepting only a few of the smallest. We see that the biblical covenants are the strong cords holding the entire Bible together.

We also note that God does everything with a purpose. History has meaning; it's going somewhere. And God is directing events so that they all arrive at his foreordained conclusion at his designated time. History and Covenant are interwoven throughout the Bible.

The Bible!—written over a period of nearly two thousand years, yet it displays a remarkable unity because of the covenants. *Once we understand the biblical covenants, we understand the Bible!*

Co-Heirs with Jesus Christ through the New Covenant

We have examined all six of the biblical covenants. The Noahic Covenant stands by itself, still in effect. The New

Covenant in Jesus Christ concludes the bilateral Mosaic Covenant and, at the same time, brings to fuller flower the other three unilateral Covenants—Abrahamic, Levitical and Davidic. The New Covenant is thus a unilateral Covenant, and it's eternal also (Hebrews 13:20,21). Its effectiveness in an individual life is conditional only upon that person's acceptance of the Covenant, by faith in Jesus Christ as his Lord. The Covenant blessings can only be rejected by man; God has bound Himself, and He will not reject us. The New Covenant has been made available to the entire human race.

> He is the expiation for our sins, and not for ours
> only but also for the sins of the whole world:
> > (1 John 2:2)

Sadly, there is the uncompromising warning of everlasting punishment for those who refuse God's kindness and mercy. In their case the death penalty for violations of the Mosaic Covenant still holds—also eternally.

Only our creative God is able to meld together such incompatible covenants so that each one is fulfilled—and its demands totally satisfied. The punishment we all deserve for our sins must be meted out—and it was—not upon us, but upon the Son of God. The death penalty for violation of the Mosaic Law has been exacted—and yet we live! Only God could do it so creatively! And so sacrificially!

We are co-heirs with Jesus Christ of all of God's love, wealth and kingdom—"heirs of God and fellow heirs with Christ" (Romans 8:17). We must not retreat again into the bondage of slavery! We have been bought with a price (1 Cor. 6:20)! God has

> . . . raised us up with him, and made us sit with
> him in the heavenly places in Christ Jesus, that in

the coming ages he might show the immeasura-
ble riches of his grace in kindness toward us in
Christ Jesus.   (Eph. 2:6,7)

We are no longer slaves, but sons and heirs, sharing our
Father's entire inheritance with Jesus Christ Himself.

A simple illustration. Tom grew up on a farm in the South,
his father's only son. As a boy, Tom hated the farm, because
he had no brothers to share the heavy workload. It was
always, "Tom, do this!" "Tom, do that!" If Tom noticed a
broken fence, he would never tell his dad, because he knew
the immediate response would be, "Well, Tom, go fix the
fence!" He hated it.

Then one day, when Tom was in his late teens, he had a
sudden revelation. "What's the matter with me? I'm the *heir*
to this farm! It's all *mine*!"

After that, Tom still wouldn't tell his dad whenever he
saw a broken fence. He fixed it! That farm belonged to him!
Tom was the sole heir.

That's what happens whenever a Christian finally dis-
covers who he is through the New Covenant in the blood
of Jesus Christ, and how powerful is the Spirit of God dwelling within him. We are seated *today* "with Him in the
heavenly places in Christ Jesus" (Eph. 2:6). "Our fellowship is with the Father and with his Son Jesus Christ" (1 John
1:3). "We have passed out of death into life" (1 John 3:14).
Of all the benefits we receive under the New Covenant, all
the others together cannot equal the blessings of eternal life.
Life for ever, in the presence of God, is incomparable.

God intends that we have his very best. He desires that
we live in his presence for ever (John 14:2,3). As Jeremiah
and Ezekiel prophesied more than two-and-a-half millennia
ago, so John the Revelator repeats their words.

"Behold, the dwelling of God is with men. He will dwell with them, and they shall be his people, and God himself will be with them; he will wipe away every tear from their eyes, and death shall be no more, neither shall there be mourning nor crying nor pain any more, for the former things have passed away."   (Rev. 21:3,4)

Your Privileges through the Blood of the New Covenant

All of the following privileges are yours through the blood of Jesus Christ, the blood of the New Covenant. Read them aloud, claim them, *receive* your privileges! Remind God, declare your privileges to others, tell yourself, tell the angels, and tell the devil! Disregard your feelings! "Let the redeemed of the Lord say so!" (Psalms 107:2).

"Through the blood of Jesus I have been redeemed from the curse of the Law!"   (Gal. 3:13)

"Through the blood of Jesus I have been released from all the sins of former generations!"
                                            (1 Peter 1:18,19)

"Through the blood of Jesus I have been redeemed from Satan's power!"   (Eph. 1:7)

"Through the blood of Jesus I have been delivered from the dominion of darkness!"
                                                  (Col. 1:13)

"Through the blood of Jesus I have been transferred to the kingdom of God's beloved Son!"
(Col. 1:13,14)

"Through the blood of Jesus I have been purchased for God!"   (Romans 3:25; 1 Cor. 6:19)

"Through the blood of Jesus I have been cleansed from all sin!"   (1 John 1:7; Rev. 1:5)

"Through the blood of Jesus I have been healed!"
(Isaiah 53:3-5; 1 Peter 2:24)

"Through the blood of Jesus I have a purified conscience!"   (Heb. 9:14)

"Through the blood of Jesus I have been brought near to God after having been far off!"
(Eph. 2:12,13)

"Through the blood of Jesus I have been reconciled to God!"   (Romans 5:9)

"Through the blood of Jesus I am justified before God!"   (Romans 3:24,25)

"Through the blood of Jesus I have confidence to approach God!"   (Heb. 10:19)

"Through the blood of Jesus I am made righteous!"   (Phil. 3:9)

"Through the blood of Jesus I am made holy and perfect!"   (Heb. 10:10,14; 13:12)

''Through the blood of Jesus I am equipped with everything I need in order to do God's will!'' (Heb. 13:20,21)

''Through the blood of Jesus I am redeemed for ever!'' (Heb. 9:12)

* * * * *

Now may the God of peace who brought again from the dead our Lord Jesus, the great shepherd of the sheep, by the blood of the eternal covenant, equip you with everything good that you may do his will, working in you that which is pleasing in his sight, through Jesus Christ; to whom be glory for ever and ever. Amen. *(Heb. 13:20,21)*